Basil

Basilisk Lizard Pet Owners Guide.

Basilisk Lizard Care, Behavior, Diet, Interaction, Costs and Health.

By

Ben Team

Table of Contents

About The Author

The author, Ben Team, is an environmental educator and author with over 16 years of professional reptile-keeping experience. Ben currently maintains www.FootstepsInTheForest.com, where he shares information, narration and observations of the natural world. When not writing about plants, animals and habitats, Ben enjoys spending time with his beautiful wife.

Foreword

Even the most mundane reptilian pet is certainly exotic when compared to a dog or cat, but some reptiles are clearly more extraordinary than others are.

For example, a small anole is certainly a much different creature than a beagle, yet it is unlikely to inspire awe or evoke images of far-off and unfamiliar lands. There is nothing wrong with this, and anoles certainly make good pets; but some reptile enthusiasts long for more unusual pets. They want something that looks like it hopped out of a dream or a sci-fi movie.

For such keepers, it is hard to go wrong with a basilisk. Medium-sized lizards of Central and South American forests, basilisks feature crests that give them just this type of out-of-this-world appearance. There is a great deal of variation in the extent and size of these crests among the living basilisk species, and males have much larger crests than females do. But some – particularly adult male plumed basilisks (*Basiliscus plumifrons*) – are amazing to behold.

Basilisks are certainly not good pets for all keepers. They rarely tolerate very much hands-on interaction with their keeper, and many will remain extremely flighty for their entire lives. In fact, simply catching your pet when it becomes necessary to maintain his cage or inspect him will often prove challenging.

Basilisks also require much larger cages than other species of similar size do, given their relatively high activity levels and tendency to flee perceived threats. They also require large water dishes, moderately high temperatures and a diverse array of foods.

However, for those with sufficient space and resources, as well as the right mindset to maintain a nervous species, basilisks can make fantastic specimens. There are few animals that look as amazing in a large, well-planted vivarium as basilisks do, and they are not a terribly common pet. This will also help set your pet apart from the droves of geckos and ball pythons living in living rooms and pet stores.

PART I: THE BASILISK LIZARD

Properly caring for any animal requires an understanding of the species and its place in the natural world. This includes digesting subjects as disparate as anatomy and ecology, diet and geography, and reproduction and physiology.

It is only by learning what your pet is, how it lives, what it does that you can achieve the primary goal of animal husbandry: Providing your pet with the highest quality of life possible.

Chapter 1: Basilisk Description and Anatomy

The basic body plan of basilisks (*Basiliscus* spp.) is similar to that of many other lizards. They have long bodies, large heads, long tails and a sprawling body posture.

However, despite these similarities, basilisks are unique-looking animals that are easy to identify on sight.

Size

Basilisks hatch from their eggs measuring approximately 3.5 inches (9 centimeters) in total length. Their tails are responsible for about 2 inches of this total length.

With access to an adequate quantity and quality of food, basilisks grow quickly and reach maturity within their second or third year of life. Most adults measure between 18 and 30 inches (45 and 75 centimeters) in total length. Adults can weigh as much as 7 ounces (200 grams), although particularly large specimens may weight slightly more than this. Basilisks are sexually dimorphic with respect to size, and males typically reach larger sizes than similarly aged females.

Color and Pattern

The four species of basilisk fall into one of two general color schemes: brown or green. The plumed basilisk (*Basiliscus plumifrons*) is primarily green (although some individuals are almost blue), while the other three species are primarily clad in brown tones. However, there is some degree of variation present, and some individuals exhibit both colors.

The lizards are also covered in a varying number of stripes, blotches and dots, which can range from blue to white to black. Additionally, some of the species possess longitudinal yellow stripes along their sides.

Body

Basilisks have elongated bodies that are slightly compressed in the vertical plane. Some males have a raised crest along their backs, which varies in size and extent from one species to the next. The crest helps to break up the outline of the lizards, allowing them to blend in with the vegetation more easily, and it also makes them appear larger, when viewed from the side.

Plumed basilisks are extraordinary looking lizards.

Head

Basilisks have moderately large, cone-shaped heads that are wide at the rear and somewhat pinched at the nose. Males often develop large jowls as they age. Most basilisks have a thin crest that sits atop the head. These crests are larger and more pronounced in males than the females.

Basilisks have medium-sized eyes, which feature muscular eyelids, which can open and close at will. The tympanum (ear drum) is clearly visible on the rear portion of the side of the lizard's head.

Because the basilisk's tympanum is located at the opening to the ear canal, rather than deep within it as it is in humans and other animals, water is not allowed to enter the canal. This is very important for an animal that spends significant periods of time in the water.

Basilisk nostrils are conspicuous, slightly elliptical openings, located on either side of the animal's snout. Their mouths are quite large, which enables them to consume relatively bulky prey items. Like most other lizards, they lack a secondary palate.

Limbs and Feet

Basilisks have four long, yet muscular legs that lie along the sides of their bodies. The legs support the body vertically when walking or climbing, but during periods of inactivity, the lizards rest on their ventral surface and splay their limbs out to the sides.

Five toes adorn each of their four feet. Basilisks have long, curved nails, which extend from the tip of each toe. These nails help them to grip the substrate and climb tree branches and other rough objects.

Vent

The vent is a transverse opening located under the base of a basilisk's tail, slightly behind the rear legs. This forms the exit point for all reproductive structures and products (eggs), as well as the end products of the digestive and renal systems.

The vent usually remains closed, and opens slightly when the lizards defecate, release urates, copulate or deposit eggs.

Tail

Basilisks have long, dorsolaterally flattened tails. The animals have some degree of control of the muscles of the tail base, but they cannot grip items with the tip of the tail. Instead, the tip of the tail simply follows behind them. However, their tails are quite helpful for propelling the lizards through the water when swimming.

Basilisks do not voluntarily jettison their tails, as some other lizards do. Those lizards who lose their tails (in whole or in part) are not capable of regenerating them.

Internal Organs

The internal anatomy of basilisks differs relatively little from that of other lizards or tetrapods in general.

Basilisks draw oxygen in through their nostrils; pipe it through the trachea and into the lungs. Here, blood exchanges carbon dioxide for oxygen, before it is pumped to the various body parts via the heart and blood vessels.

While the basilisk's heart features only three true chambers (two atria and a single ventricle), a septum keeps the ventricle divided at most times, allowing the heart to operate similarly to a four-chambered, mammalian heart. This means that in practice, basilisks keep their oxygenated and deoxygenated blood relatively separate in the heart.

Their digestive system is comprised of an esophagus, stomach, small intestine, large intestine and a terminal chamber called the cloaca. The stomach has some ability to stretch to accommodate food.

The liver resides near the center of the animal's torso, with the gall bladder sitting directly behind it. While the gall bladder stores bile, the liver performs a number of functions relating to digestion, metabolism and filtration. Kidneys, which lie almost directly behind the lungs, filter wastes from the lizard's bloodstream.

Like other lizards, basilisks control their bodies via their brain and nervous system. Their endocrine and exocrine glands work much as they do in other vertebrates.

Reproductive Organs

Like all squamates, male basilisks have paired reproductive organs, called hemipenes. When not in use, males keep their hemipenes inside the bases of their tails. When they attempt to mate with a female, they evert one of the hemipenes and insert it into the female's cloaca.

The paired nature of the male sex organs ensures that males can continue to breed if they suffer injury to one of the hemipenes. This paired arrangement also allows male basilisks to mate with females on either side of their body.

Females have paired ovaries, which produce ova (eggs), and they have paired oviducts, which store the eggs after they are released from the ovaries. The eggs are shelled and held inside the oviducts until it is time to deposit the eggs. At this time, the eggs are passed from the oviducts into the cloaca and out of the body via the vent.

Chapter 2: Basilisk Biology and Behavior

Basilisks exhibit several biological and behavioral adaptations that allow them to survive in their natural habitats.

Shedding

Like other scaled reptiles, basilisks shed their old skin to reveal new, fresh skin underneath. However, these lizards do not shed their skin in one piece, as most snakes do. Instead, they tend to shed in several separate pieces over the course of a day or two.

Basilisks may consume their shed skin, but this is not as common a phenomenon as it is in some other lizards, such as geckos.

Metabolism and Digestion

Basilisks are ectothermic ("cold-blooded") animals, whose internal metabolism depends on their body temperature. When warm, their bodily functions proceed more rapidly; when cold, their bodily functions proceed slowly.

This also means that the lizards digest more effectively at suitably warm temperatures than they do at suboptimal temperatures. Their appetites also vary with temperature, and if the temperatures drop below the preferred range, they may cease feeding entirely.

A basilisk's body temperature largely follows ambient air temperatures, but they also absorb and reflect radiant heat, such as that coming from the sun. The lizards try to keep their body temperature within the preferred range by employing behaviors that allow them adjust their temperature.

For example, basilisks bask to raise their temperature when they are too cool. This typically involves orienting their body so that they are perpendicular with the sun's rays. Additionally, some individuals may exhibit darker colors when basking or flatten their bodies to help absorb more infrared rays.

By contrast, when it is necessary to cool off, basilisks may move into the shade, dive into the water or gape their mouths to release excess heat.

Growth Rate and Lifespan

Basilisks grow quickly during their first year of life, but this growth rate slows in their second and subsequent years. Nevertheless, there is a great deal of variation in individual growth rates, and invariably some clutch mates grow much more quickly or slowly than their siblings do. This can lead some lizards to be twice the size of their siblings by their first birthday.

Most basilisks should reach sexual maturity by the time they are two or three years of age, although some will take longer. The lizards continue to grow after becoming mature, although this growth rate is especially slow.

Hatchling basilisks are consumed by a wide variety of predators, but those that reach maturity are capable of reaching about 10 years of age in the wild. However, in captivity, where the lizards are provided with unlimited food, veterinary care and protection from parasites and predators, they may live much longer than this.

Foraging Behavior

Basilisks employ two primary foraging modes: They actively hunt for food and they ambush passing prey items as the opportunity arises.

Basilisks primarily rely on their sense of vision to locate prey and edible plants, but they may taste potential food items (particularly plant-based foods) with their fleshy tongue before consuming them.

Basilisks spend a lot of time in the wild resting on elevated perches, particularly those above the water. If they spot a potential prey item scurrying by they will descend and travel several feet to capture it. At times, they will enter the water to pursue aquatic prey.

Diel and Seasonal Activity

Basilisks are almost entirely diurnal animals, who spend their days basking in the sun, foraging for food, seeking mates and defending themselves from predators.

With the onset of night, most basilisks find a safe place to sleep until dawn. Many sleep on exposed perches, but other individuals find a rock crevice, burrow or patch of dense vegetation in which they remain throughout the night.

Basilisks are active throughout the year, but their breeding activity is concentrated in the rainy season.

Defensive Strategies and Tactics

Crypsis is the first method by which basilisks seek to defend themselves. The combination of their camouflaged colors, flattened body, sedentary behavior and crests makes them blend in quite well in their natural habitats.

When crypsis fails, basilisks often head for the water. While they may dive into the water and swim for safety, they may also run straight across the surface of the water. This behavior, for which they are quite famous, has earned them the name "Jesus Lizard," among some. They are quite effective swimmers and they can remain submerged for long periods of time, so this strategy works well for the lizards.

If unable to escape danger, basilisks may stand their ground and face the threat. They may arch their backs, gape their mouths, lash their tails or expand their bodies to appear larger. If these tactics fail to deter the threat, they will resort to biting, thrashing and defecating on the predator.

While their teeth are relatively small, large basilisks can inflict a rather strong pinch with their jaws. The bites from small basilisks are harmless, and unlikely to deter most predators.

Reproduction

Basilisks may mate and lay eggs during any portion of the year, but most reproductive activity occurs during the rainy season (broadly defined as April to December).

Males will usually attempt to breed with any females that pass through their territory. But because females do not always acquiesce to such advances, these encounters often appear violent. Males may repeatedly bite the females on the raised dorsal crest to hold them in place.

Over the course of a breeding season, males may mate with several females. Females may mate with more than one male, but they can retain the sperm from a single mating and deposit multiple clutches of eggs over the course of the breeding season.

As the time for egg deposition nears, the females excavate a small egg chamber in the soil, often at the base of a tree, shrub or rock. Once completed, the female will turn around and deposit between 10 and 15 eggs.

The female will cover the egg chamber upon completing parturition. Once she leaves, she will have no further contact with the young. Basilisks provide no care for the hatchlings, and may even predate upon them.

The young begin hatching from their eggs about one to three months after deposition, depending upon the temperatures in the egg chamber. They may remain in their shells for a day or two, but soon, they will dig their way out of the soil.

Chapter 3: Classification and Taxonomy

Basilisks are a well-defined group of lizards, who all spring from a common ancestor. While their taxonomy has been subject to a few revisions, there is no doubt that these lizards represent a distinct lineage, compromised of a handful of different species.

But before delving more deeply into the classification and taxonomy of basilisks, it is helpful to begin with a broader context.

Although the taxonomy of lizards is the subject of great debate, the Integrated Taxonomic Information System currently classifies all of the living basilisks in the subfamily Polychrotinae, which is part of the Iguanidae family.

Polychrotinae contains several different genera that are close relatives of the basilisks. A few of the most important genera include *Anolis*, *Polychrus* and *Norops*. Basilisks are all members of the genus *Basciliscus*.

Most authorities recognize four species within the genus *Basiliscus*: the common basilisk (*Basiliscus basiliscus*), the red-headed basilisk (*Basiliscus galeritus*), the plumed basilisk (*Basiliscus plumifrons*) and the striped basilisk (*Basiliscus vittatus*).

Each of these species possesses unique traits, but they are all medium-sized lizards with broadly similar morphology. No subspecies are recognized among any of these species.

The striped basilisk, common basilisk and plumed basilisk are the ones most commonly seen in captive collection.

Chapter 4: The Basilisk's World

Basilisks have evolved to survive in their natural habitat over millions of years. Accordingly, you must understand their native habitat – and provide a reasonable facsimile of it – to maintain these lizards successfully.

Range and Habitat

Basilisks range throughout the tropical portions of the New World, from southern Mexico in the north to Ecuador and Venezuela in the south. Additionally, although they are not native to the United States, basilisks have been introduced to south Florida. They've managed to establish permanent, reproductively viable colonies in several areas in the southern part of the state.

Basilisks typically inhabit tropical rainforests. They are primarily lizards of lowlands, but some species inhabit forests as high as 5,000 feet (1,500 meters) above sea level. Basilisks are rarely found very far from water, and they are most common in riparian areas. Living in such close proximity to water not only ensures plenty of prey are available, but it provides the lizards with a place to which they can flee if threatened by a predator.

Climate

Temperatures within the natural range of basilisks are relatively warm year-round. Daytime high temperatures in July and August may approach 100 degrees Fahrenheit (37 degrees Celsius), while those in January usually reach into the low 80s Fahrenheit (26 degrees Celsius). Such temperatures permit the lizards to be active throughout the year, even though nighttime temperatures can drop into the high 60s Fahrenheit (20 degrees Celsius) during winter nights.

Annual precipitation throughout the range of basilisks varies from about 40 to 120 inches (100 to 300 centimeters) per year, depending on the specific location in question. Although the seasonal variation in rainfall varies from one location to the next, the primary rainy season for the region encompasses the time between April or May and December. Some locations experience very distinct wet and dry seasons.

Natural Diet

Basilisks eat a wide variety of foods, including insects, vertebrates and plant matter. They are consummate generalists, who will adapt to whatever prey is abundant in their area. Insects (and other invertebrates) are undoubtedly the most important class of prey taken, but no small animal is safe from the jaws of a hungry basilisk.

Some of the primary invertebrate clades that basilisks prey upon include:

- Lepidopterans (adult butterflies, moths, skippers and larvae)

- Coleopterans (adult beetles and larvae)

- Dipterans (adult flies, crane flies, mosquitoes and larvae)

- Orthopterans (grasshoppers, katydids and crickets)

- Mollusks (snails and slugs)

- Annelids (earthworms)

- Arachnids (spiders and harvestmen)

Additionally, basilisks have been known to consume small lizards, snakes, frogs and fish. Most of the plant matter they consume consists of flowers, fruits and seeds, although leaves and stems were included among the stomach contents of some wild specimens. (Fitch, 1974)

Natural Predators

Virtually every medium-sized predator that shares habitat with basilisks represents a potential threat. This includes snakes, larger lizards, birds of prey and mammalian predators, such as weasels, opossums and small cats. Basilisks may even be in danger from larger individuals of their own species.

However, as with most other animals, the greatest threat basilisks face in the wild is habitat destruction. However, collection for the pet trade also represents a significant check on their populations.

PART II: BASILISK HUSBANDRY

Once equipped with a basic understanding of what basilisks *are* (Chapter 1 and Chapter 3), where they *live* (Chapter 4), and what they *do* (Chapter 2) you can begin learning about their captive care.

Animal husbandry is an evolving pursuit. Keepers shift their strategies frequently as they incorporate new information and ideas into their husbandry paradigms.

There are few "right" or "wrong" answers, and what works in one situation may not work in another. Accordingly, you may find that different authorities present different, and sometimes conflicting, information regarding the care of these lizards.

In all cases, you must strive to learn as much as you can about your pet and its natural habitat, so that you may provide it with the best quality of life possible.

Chapter 5: Basilisks as Pets

Basilisks can make rewarding pets, but you must know what to expect before adding one to your home and family. This includes not only understanding the nature of the care they require, but also the costs associated with this care.

Assuming that you feel confident in your ability to care for a basilisk and endure the associated financial burdens, you can begin seeking your individual pet.

Understanding the Commitment

Keeping a basilisk as a pet requires a substantial commitment. You will be responsible for your pet's well-being for the rest of its life. Although basilisks are not particularly long-lived animals, their lifespans are not trivial.

Can you be sure that you will still want to care for your pet several years in the future? Do you know what your living situation will be? What changes will have occurred in your family? How will your working life have changed over this time?

You must consider all of these possibilities before acquiring a new pet. Failing to do so often leads to apathy, neglect and even resentment, which is not good for you or your pet lizard.

Neglecting your pet is wrong, and in some locations, a criminal offense. You must continue to provide quality care for your basilisk, even once the novelty has worn off, and it is no longer fun to clean the cage and purchase crickets a few times a week.

Once you purchase a basilisk, its well-being becomes your responsibility until it passes away at the end of a long life, or you have found someone who will agree to adopt the animal for you.

Unfortunately, this is rarely an easy task. You may begin with thoughts of selling your pet to help recoup a small part of your investment, but these efforts will largely fall flat.

While professional breeders may profit from the sale of basilisks, amateurs are at a decided disadvantage. Only a tiny sliver of the general population is interested in reptilian pets, and only a small subset of these are interested in keeping basilisks.

Of those who are interested in acquiring a basilisk, most would rather start fresh, by *purchasing* a small hatchling or juvenile from an established breeder, rather than adopting your questionable animal *for free*.

After having difficulty finding a willing party to purchase or adopt your animal, many owners try to donate their pet to a local zoo. Unfortunately, this rarely works either. Zoos are not interested in your pet lizard, no matter how pretty he is and how readily he snatches crickets from your fingers. He is a pet with little to no reliable provenance and questionable health status. This is simply not the type of animal zoos are eager to add to their multi-million dollar collections.

Zoos obtain most of their animals from other zoos and museums; failing that, they obtain their animals directly from their land of origin. As a rule, they do not accept donated pets.

No matter how difficult it becomes to find a new home for your unwanted basilisk, you must never release non-native reptiles into the wild. Basilisks can colonize places outside their native range, with disastrous results for the ecosystem's native fauna.

Additionally, released or escaped reptiles cause a great deal of distress to those who are frightened by them. This leads local municipalities to adopt pet restrictions or ban reptile keeping entirely. While the chances of an escaped or released basilisk harming anyone are very low, it is unlikely that those who fear reptiles will see the threat as minor.

The Costs of Captivity
Reptiles are often marketed as low-cost pets. While true in a relative sense (the costs associated with dog, cat, horse or tropical fish husbandry are often much higher than they are for basilisks), potential keepers must still prepare for the financial implications of basilisk ownership.

At the outset, you must budget for the acquisition of your pet, as well as the costs of purchasing or constructing a habitat. Unfortunately, while many keepers plan for these costs, they typically fail to consider the on-going costs, which will quickly eclipse the initial startup costs.

Startup Costs
One surprising fact most new keepers learn is the enclosure and equipment will often cost more than the animal does (except in the case of very high-priced specimens).

Striped basilisks camouflage well with their surroundings.

Prices fluctuate from one market to the next, but in general, the least you will spend on a single basilisk is about $25 (£20), while the least you will spend on the *initial* habitat and assorted equipment will be about $50 (£40). Replacement equipment and food will represent additional (and ongoing) expenses.

Examine the charts on the following pages to get an idea of three different pricing scenarios. While the specific prices listed will vary based on innumerable factors, the charts are instructive for first-time buyers.

The first scenario details a budget-minded keeper, trying to spend as little as possible. The second example estimates the costs for a keeper with a moderate budget, and the third example provides a case study for extravagant shoppers, who want an expensive basilisk and top-notch equipment.

These charts are only provided estimates; your experience may vary based on a variety of factors.

Inexpensive Option

Hatchling Basilisk	$25 (£20)
Economy Homemade Habitat	$25 (£20)
Heat Lamp or Heating Pad	$20 (£16)
Plants, Substrate, Hides, etc.	$20 (£16)
Infrared Thermometer	$35 (£24)
Digital Indoor-Outdoor Thermometer	$20 (£16)
Water Dish, Forceps, Spray Bottles, Misc.	$20 (£16)
Total	**$165 (£128)**

Moderate Option

Adult Basilisk	$100 (£80)
Premium Homemade Habitat	$100 (£80)
Heat Lamp or Heating Pad	$20 (£16)
Plants, Substrate, Hides, etc.	$20 (£16)
Infrared Thermometer	$35 (£24)
Digital Indoor-Outdoor Thermometer	$20 (£16)
Water Dish, Forceps, Spray Bottles, Misc.	$20 (£16)
Total	**$315 (£248)**

Premium Option

Premium Basilisk	$300 (£240)
Premium Commercial Cage	$200 (£160)
Heat Lamp or Heating Pad	$20 (£16)
Plants, Substrate, Hides, etc.	$20 (£16)
Infrared Thermometer	$35 (£24)
Digital Indoor-Outdoor Thermometer	$20 (£16)
Water Dish, Forceps, Spray Bottles, Misc.	$20 (£16)
Total	**$615 (£500)**

Ongoing Costs

The ongoing costs of basilisk ownership primarily fall into one of three categories: food, maintenance and veterinary care.

Food costs are the most significant of the three, but they are relatively consistent and somewhat predictable. Some maintenance costs are easy to calculate, but things like equipment malfunctions are impossible to predict with any certainty. Veterinary expenses are hard to predict and vary wildly from one year to the next.

Food Costs

Food is the single greatest ongoing cost you will experience while caring for your basilisk. To obtain a reasonable estimate of your yearly food costs, you must consider the number of meals you will feed your pet per year and the cost of each meal.

The amount of food your basilisk will consume will vary based on numerous factors, including his size, the average temperatures in his habitat and his health.

As a ballpark number, you should figure that you'll need about $5 (£4) per week – roughly $250 (£205) per year -- for food. You could certainly spend more or less than this, but that is a reasonable estimate for back-of-the-envelope calculations.

Veterinary Costs

While you should always seek veterinary advice at the first sign of illness, it is probably not wise to haul your healthy basilisk to the vet's office for no reason – they don't require "checkups" or annual vaccinations as some other pets may. Accordingly, you shouldn't incur any veterinary expenses unless your pet falls ill.

However, veterinary care can become very expensive, very quickly. In addition to a basic exam or phone consultation, your lizard may need cultures, x-rays or other diagnostic tests performed. In light of this, wise keepers budget at least $200 to $300 (£160 to £245) each year to cover any emergency veterinary costs.

Maintenance Costs

It is important to plan for both routine and unexpected maintenance costs. Commonly used items, such as paper towels, disinfectant and top soil are rather easy to calculate. However, it is not easy to know how many burned out light bulbs, cracked misting units or faulty thermostats you will have to replace in a given year.

Those who keep their basilisks in simple enclosures will find that about $50 (£40) covers their yearly maintenance costs. By contrast, those who maintain elaborate habitats may spend $200 (£160) or more each year. Always try to purchase frequently used supplies, such as light bulbs, paper towels and disinfectants in bulk to maximize your savings.

Myths and Misunderstandings

Myth: Lizards that shed their tails will readily produce a replacement tail.

Fact: Most lizards that autotomize their tails grow a replacement tail. However, basilisks do not have fracture planes in their tails, so they do not detach easily, nor do they re-grow if they break. Accordingly, it is important that you never lift your basilisk by the tail.

Myth: Basilisks need "friends" or they will get lonely.

Fact: Although they can be kept in small groups, consisting of two or three females and a single male, basilisks are essentially solitary animals in the wild, who spend the bulk of their lives alone. Accordingly, they will never "miss" having cagemates, and you should not feel obligated to keep them in a communal setting.

Myth: Reptiles grow in proportion to the size of their cage and then stop.

Fact: Reptiles do no such thing. Most healthy lizards, snakes and turtles grow throughout their lives, although the rate of growth slows with age (some stop growing with maturity, although this is not influenced by the size of their cage).

Placing them in a small cage in an attempt to stunt their growth is an unthinkably cruel practice, which is more likely to sicken or kill your pet than stunt its growth.

Providing a basilisk with an inadequately spacious cage is a sure recipe for illness, maladaptation and eventual death.

Myth: Basilisks must eat live food.

Fact: Most basilisks – in fact, most insectivorous lizards – require live insects for food. However, some hobbyists have had success teaching their basilisks to accept pre-killed insects (such as are occasionally sold in pet stores) or pre-killed rodents offered via forceps.

Myth: Reptiles have no emotions and do not suffer.

Fact: While basilisks have very primitive brains and do not have emotions comparable to those of higher mammals, they can absolutely suffer. Always treat reptiles with the same compassion you would offer a dog, cat or horse.

Myth: Basilisks are tame lizards that never bite.

Fact: While basilisks are generally disinclined to bite, there is nothing precluding them from doing so. Large basilisks can inflict a relatively painful pinch, should they decide to bite, and they may break the skin.

Acquiring Your Basilisk

Modern reptile enthusiasts can acquire basilisks from a variety of sources, each with a different set of pros and cons.

Pet stores are one of the first places many people see basilisks, and they become the de facto source of pets for many beginning keepers. While they do offer some unique benefits to prospective keepers, pet stores are not always the best place to purchase a basilisk; so, consider all of the available options, including breeders and reptile swap meets, before making a purchase.

Pet Stores

Pet stores offer a number of benefits to keepers shopping for basilisks, including convenience: They usually stock all of the equipment your new lizard needs, including cages, heating devices and food items.

Additionally, they offer you the chance to inspect the lizard up close before purchase. In some cases, you may be able to choose from more than one specimen. Many pet stores provide health guarantees for a short period, that provides some recourse if your new pet turns out to be ill.

However, pet stores are not always the ideal place to purchase your new pet. Pet stores are retail establishments, and as such, you will usually pay more for your new pet than you would from a breeder.

Additionally, pet stores rarely know the pedigree of the animals they sell, and they will rarely know the lizard's date of birth, or other pertinent information. Only a handful of pet stores will be able to distinguish among the various basilisk species, so specimens may also be mislabeled.

Other drawbacks associated with pet stores primarily relate to the staff's inexperience. While some pet stores concentrate on reptiles and may educate their staff about proper basilisk care, many others provide incorrect advice to their customers.

It is also worth considering the increased exposure to pathogens that pet store animals endure, given the constant flow of animals through such facilities.

Reptile Expos

Reptile expos offer another option for purchasing a basilisk. Reptile expos often feature resellers, breeders and retailers in the same room, all selling various types of basilisks and other reptiles.

Often, the prices at such events are quite reasonable and you are often able to select from many different lizards. However, if you have a problem, it may be difficult to find the seller after the event is over.

Breeders

Because they usually offer unparalleled information and support to their customers, breeders are generally the best place for most novices to shop for basilisks. Additionally, breeders often know the species well, and are better able to help you learn the husbandry techniques necessary for success.

For those seeking a truly spectacular basilisk, breeders are often the only option. The same principle holds true for those seeking individuals from proven bloodlines – the only place to purchase such basilisks are from breeders.

The primary disadvantage of buying from a breeder is that you must often make such purchases from a distance, either by phone or via the internet. Nevertheless, most established breeders are happy to provide you with photographs of the animal you will be purchasing, as well as his or her parents.

Selecting Your Basilisk

Not all basilisks are created equally, so it is important to select a healthy individual that will give you the best chance of success.

Practically speaking, the most important criterion to consider is the health of the animal. However, the sex, age and history of the lizard are also important things to consider.

Health Checklist

Always check your basilisk thoroughly for signs of injury or illness before purchasing it. If you are purchasing the animal from someone in a different part of the country, you must inspect it immediately upon delivery. Notify the seller promptly if the animal exhibits any health problems.

Avoid the temptation to acquire or accept a sick or injured animal in hopes of nursing him back to health. Not only are you likely to incur substantial veterinary costs while treating your new pet, you will likely fail in your attempts to restore the lizard to full health. Sick basilisks rarely recover in the hands of novices.

Additionally, by purchasing injured or diseased animals, you incentivize poor husbandry on the part of the retailer. If retailers lose money on sick or injured animals, they will take steps to avoid this eventuality, by acquiring healthier stock in the first place, and providing better care for their charges.

As much as is possible, try to observe the following features:

- **Observe the lizard's skin**. It should be free of lacerations and other damage. Pay special attention to those areas that frequently sustain damage, such as the tip of the lizard's tail, the toes and the tip of the snout. A small cut or abrasion may be relatively easy to treat, but significant abrasions and cuts are likely to become infected and require significant treatment.

- **Gently check the lizard's crevices and creases for mites and ticks**. Mites are about the size of a flake of pepper, and they may be black, brown or red. Mites often move about on the lizard, whereas ticks – if attached and feeding – do not move. Avoid purchasing any animal that has either parasite. Additionally, you should avoid purchasing any other animals from this source, as they are likely to harbor parasites as well.

- **Examine the lizard's eyes, ears and nostrils**. The eyes should not be sunken, and they should be free of discharge. The nostrils should be clear and dry – lizards with runny noses or those who blow bubbles are likely to be suffering from a respiratory infection. However, be aware that lizards often get some water in their nostrils while drinking water. This is no cause for concern.

- **Gently palpate the animal and ensure no lumps or anomalies are apparent**. Lumps in the muscles or abdominal cavity may indicate parasites, abscesses or tumors.

- **Observe the lizard's demeanor**. Healthy lizards are aware of their environment and react to stimuli. When active, the lizard should calmly explore his environment. While you may wish to avoid purchasing an aggressive, defensive or flighty animal, these behaviors do not necessarily indicate a health problem.

- **Check the lizard's vent**. The vent should be clean and free of smeared feces. Smeared feces can indicate parasites or bacterial infections.

- **Check the lizard's appetite**. If possible, ask the retailer to feed the lizard a cricket, superworm or roach. A healthy basilisk should usually exhibit a strong food drive, although failing to eat is not *necessarily* a bad sign – the lizard may not be hungry.

The Age
Hatchling basilisks are very fragile until they reach about one month of age. Before this, they are unlikely to thrive in the hands of beginning keepers.

Accordingly, most beginners should purchase two- or three-month-old juveniles, who have already become well established. Animals of this age tolerate the changes associated with a new home better than very young specimens do. Further, given their greater size, they will better tolerate temperature and humidity extremes than smaller animals will.

Mature animals can make acceptable pets, but they may intimidate new keepers.

The Sex
Unless you are attempting to breed basilisks, you should select a male pet, as females are more likely to suffer from reproduction-related health problems than males are. Additionally, males are generally more visually impressive and have larger crests.

Most females will produce and deposit egg clutches upon reaching maturity, whether they are housed with a male or not. While this is not necessarily problematic, novices can easily avoid this unnecessary complication by selecting males as pets.

Quarantine
Because new animals may have illnesses or parasites that could infect the rest of your collection, it is wise to quarantine all new acquisitions. This means that you should keep any new animal as separated from the rest of your pets as possible. Only once you have ensured that the new animal is healthy should you introduce it to the rest of your collection.

During the quarantine period, you should keep the new lizard in a simplified habitat, with a paper substrate, water bowl, basking spot and a few hiding places. Keep the temperature and humidity at ideal levels.

It is wise to obtain fecal samples from your lizard during the quarantine period. You can take these samples to your veterinarian, who can check them for signs of internal parasites. Always treat any existing parasite infestations before removing the animal from quarantine.

Always tend to quarantined animals last, as this reduces the chances of transmitting pathogens to your healthy animals. Do not wash quarantined water bowls or cage furniture with those belonging to your healthy animals. Whenever possible, use completely separate tools for quarantined animals and those that have been in your collection for some time.

Always be sure to wash your hands thoroughly after handling quarantined animals, their cages or their tools. Particularly careful keepers wear a smock or alternative clothing when handling quarantined animals.

Quarantine new acquisitions for a minimum of 30 days; 60 or 90 days is even better. Many zoos and professional breeders maintain 180- or 360-day-long quarantine periods.

Chapter 6: Providing the Captive Habitat

In most respects, providing your new basilisk with a suitable captive habitat requires that you functionally replicate the various aspects of their wild habitats.

In most respects, providing basilisks with a suitable captive habitat entails *functionally* replicating the various aspects of their wild habitats. In other words, the habitat needn't *look* like lush Cambodian jungle, but it must *function* like one.

After providing your pet with an enclosure (this chapter), you will need to provide the animal with the correct thermal environment (Chapter 7), the correct lighting (Chapter 8), and the correct substrate and cage furniture (Chapter 9).

Enclosure

Providing your basilisk with appropriate housing is and essential aspect of captive care. In essence, the habitat you provide to your pet becomes his entire world.

In "the old days," those inclined to keep reptiles had few choices with regard to caging. The two primary options were to build a custom cage from scratch or construct a lid to use with a fish aquarium.

By contrast, modern hobbyists have a variety of options from which to choose. In addition to building custom cages or adapting aquaria, dozens of different cage styles are available – each with different pros and cons.

Remember: There are few absolutes regarding reptile husbandry, and what works for most keepers and lizards may not work for you and your pet. Additionally, advanced keepers are often able to sidestep problems that trouble beginners, which means that they can break some of the "rules" that apply to fledgling keepers.

The most commonly used enclosure styles include aquariums, commercial cages, custom-built cages and modified plastic storage containers.

Aquariums

Aquariums are popular choices for many pet reptiles and they are available at virtually every pet store in the country. However, they present several challenges for basilisk maintenance and are not ideal for this purpose.

While many 10- and 20-gallon aquariums have footprints that are acceptable for housing very small basilisks, few aquariums are manufactured in the appropriate layout for adults. While small aquariums have a large footprint relative to their volume, large aquariums have small footprints relative to their volume. This is because they are designed for fish rather than reptiles, who use their available space in different ways.

Also, aquariums are built so that the top of the enclosure serves as the opening, rather than the front. This can make it difficult to access the animal or clean the enclosure if the heat lamps and full-spectrum bulbs are resting on top of the cage.

Aquariums are also heavy. Large aquariums – particularly those loaded with substrate, rocks and perches -- are very heavy. Most will require two people to lift and move. Additionally, the glass construction makes aquariums very fragile enclosures, which can break very easily.

One final problem with aquariums that specifically relates to the maintenance of basilisks, is the use of glass for the cage walls. Basilisks often react to threats by immediately running at full speed in just about any direction imaginable. This often causes them to slam into the cage glass, causing themselves serious injuries. If you do use an aquarium for basilisk maintenance, you must paint or cover the bottom portion of the glass with something opaque to prevent this from happening.

Commercial Cages
Commercially produced reptile enclosures (such as those designed for snakes) are widely regarded as the best choice for basilisk maintenance.

Most commercial cages are made from plastic or glass, and they feature doors on the front of the enclosure, rather than on the top. This means that they provide better access to the enclosure than aquariums do. Additionally, commercial reptile cages usually feature better footprint-to-volume ratios than aquariums do.

Commercial cages are usually sturdier than glass aquariums and lighter too. This makes them much easier to handle and move than aquariums.

Custom Built Cages
For keepers with access to tools and the desire and skill to use them, it is possible to construct homemade cages.

A number of materials are suitable for cage construction, and each has different pros and cons. Wood is commonly used, but must be adequately sealed to avoid rotting, warping or absorbing offensive odors.

Plastic sheeting is a very good material, but few have the necessary skills, knowledge and tools necessary for cage construction. Additionally, some plastics may have extended off-gassing times.

Glass can be used (although as with aquariums, this presents specific problems for basilisks), whether glued to itself or when used with a frame. Custom-built glass cages can be better than aquariums, as you can design them in dimensions that are appropriate for basilisks. Additionally, they can be constructed in such a way that the door is on the front of the cage, rather than the top.

In all cases, the cages should be designed to contain the lizard safely, provide an adequate amount of floor space and allow the keeper suitable access.

Plastic Storage Containers
Plastic storage containers, such as those used for shoes, sweaters or food, can make sufficient enclosures for basilisks.

While they are not particularly pretty, plastic storage boxes offer a number of advantages over other cage styles. This is especially true when housing small lizards.

For example, plastic storage boxes are much lighter than either aquariums or commercial cages, and they are less likely to break. Plastic storage containers are almost always much cheaper than cages or aquariums of similar size.

Usually, in order for plastic storage containers to serve as convenient housing, they must be tall enough to contain the lizards without the need for a lid. Obviously, this is not advisable in homes with pets or small children.

Plastic containers are rarely available in sizes appropriate for large adult basilisks, but enterprising keepers may use cattle stock tanks or prefabricated pond liners instead.

Outdoor Enclosures
Outdoor enclosures are great for giving your basilisk access to natural sunlight. While most keepers will only be able to do so during the warmest portions of the year, those living in southern Florida or California may be able to keep basilisks outdoors year-round.

To house your basilisk outdoors, you will need to erect a boundary of some type, constructed from either wood, stone, concrete or plastic planks.

To keep the local predators from consuming your pets, you will need to place a screen or fence over the top of the enclosure.

Bury a short length of chain-link fencing or robust screen around the periphery of the enclosure to ensure digging predators cannot gain access to the cage.

You will need to place the enclosure in a place that receives adequate sunshine, so the lizards can bask and raise their body temperature effectively. However, the lizards must have access to shade, particularly during the middle of the day, as basilisks do not relish strong sunlight as much as other agamids do.

Dimensions

Basilisks require a fair bit of space to thrive. Minimally, each adult should have about 8 to 10 square feet (0.75 to 1 square meter) of floor space in the enclosure. However, it is preferable to provide more than this – particularly when housing adults. These are active lizards, who almost always benefit from the largest cages possible. Closet- or room-sized enclosures are ideal.

Hatchlings and juveniles require less space than adults do. Basilisks between 4 and 8 inches in length are comfortable in about 2 square feet (0.2 square meters) of space. You can use an intermediate cage for lizards between 8 and 12 inches in length, with about 4 square feet (0.4 square meters) of space, but it is more economical to simply skip the intermediate cage and move lizards of this size into their adult, permanent enclosures.

Basilisks require relatively tall cages in order to thrive. Minimally, you must provide at least 24 inches (60 centimeters) of cage height, but twice or thrice this much height is preferable.

Basilisks are essentially solitary lizards in the wild, but given enough space, they often adjust to communal living arrangements. However, mature males should not be housed together, as they are likely to engage in brutal physical confrontations, which can leave them injured and stressed.

Chapter 7: Establishing the Thermal Environment

Providing the proper thermal environment is one of the most important aspects of reptile husbandry. As ectothermic ("cold blooded") animals, basilisks rely on the surrounding temperatures to regulate the rate at which their metabolism operates.

Providing a proper thermal environment can mean the difference between a healthy, thriving basilisk and one who spends a great deal of time at the veterinarian's office, battling infections and illness.

While individuals may demonstrate slightly different preferences, basilisks generally prefer ambient temperatures in the low-80s Fahrenheit (about 27 to 30 degrees Celsius), with access to a basking spot or warm area in the cage that offers temperatures in the mid-90s Fahrenheit (34 to 35 degrees Celsius).

Providing your basilisk with a suitable thermal environment requires the correct approach, the correct heating equipment and the tools necessary for monitoring the thermal environment.

Size-Related Heating Concerns

Before examining the best way to establish a proper thermal environment, it is important to understand that your lizard's body size influences the way in which he heats up and cools off.

Because volume increases more quickly than surface area does with increasing body size, small individuals experience more rapid temperature fluctuations than larger individuals do.

This principle is an especially important factor to keep in mind when caring for hatchling and juvenile basilisks: Thermal stress affects such lizards quickly, and excessively high or low temperatures often prove fatal.

Accordingly, it is imperative to protect small individuals from temperature extremes. Conversely, larger basilisks are more tolerant of temperature extremes than smaller individuals are (though they should still be protected from temperature extremes).

Thermal Gradients

In the wild, basilisks move between different microhabitats so that they can maintain ideal body temperature as much as possible. You want to provide similar opportunities for your captive lizard by creating a thermal gradient.

The best way to do this is by clustering the heating devices at one end of the habitat, thereby creating a basking spot (the warmest spot in the enclosure).

The temperatures will slowly drop with increasing distance from the basking spot, which creates a *gradient* of temperatures. This mimics the way temperatures vary from one small place to the next in your pet's natural habitat. For example, a wild basilisk may move under the tree canopy to escape the sun, or move out onto a sun-bathed rock to heat up on a cool morning.

By establishing a gradient in the enclosure, your captive basilisk will be able to access a range of different temperatures, which will allow him to manage his body temperature just as his wild counterparts do.

Adjust the heating device until the surface temperatures at the basking spot are between 90 and 95 degrees Fahrenheit (32 to 35 degrees Celsius). Because there is no heat source at the other end of the cage, the ambient temperature will gradually fall as your lizard moves away from the heat source. Ideally, the cool end of the cage should be in the high-70s Fahrenheit (24 to 26 degrees Celsius).

The need to establish a thermal gradient is one of the most compelling reasons to use a large cage. In general, the larger the cage, the easier it is to establish a suitable thermal gradient.

Heating Equipment
There are a variety of different heating devices you can use to keep your basilisk's habitat within the appropriate temperature range. Be sure to consider your choice carefully, and select the best type of heating device for you and your lizard.

Heat Lamps
Heat lamps are one of the best ways to heat your basilisk's habitat. Heat lamps consist of a reflector dome and an incandescent bulb. The light bulb produces heat (in addition to light) and the metal reflector dome directs the heat to a spot inside the cage.

You will need to clamp the lamp to a stable anchor or part of the cage's frame. Always be sure that the lamp is securely attached and will not be dislodged by vibration, children or pets.

Because fire safety is always a concern, and many keepers use high-wattage lightbulbs, opt for heavy-duty reflector domes with ceramic bases, rather than economy units with plastic bases. The price difference is negligible, given the stakes.

One of the greatest benefits of using heat lamps to maintain the temperature of your pet's habitat is the flexibility they offer. While you can adjust the amount of heat provided by heat tapes and other devices with a rheostat or thermostat, you can adjust the enclosure temperature provided by heat lamps in two ways:

- **Changing the Bulb Wattage**

The simplest way to adjust the temperature of your basilisk's cage is by changing the wattage of the bulb you are using.

For example, if a 40-watt light bulb is not raising the temperature of the basking spot high enough, you may try a 60-watt bulb. Alternatively, if a 100-watt light bulb is elevating the cage temperatures higher than are appropriate, switching to a 60-watt bulb may help.

- **Adjusting the Distance between the Heat Lamp and the Basking Spot**

The closer the heat lamp is to the cage, the warmer the cage will be. If the habitat is too warm, you can move the light farther from the enclosure, which should lower the basking spot temperatures slightly.

However, the farther away you move the lamp, the larger the basking spot becomes. It is important to be careful that you do not move it to far away, which will reduce the effectiveness of the thermal gradient by heating the enclosure too uniformly. In very large cages, this may not compromise the thermal gradient very much, but in a small cage, it may eliminate the "cool side" of the habitat.

In other words, if your heat lamp creates a basking spot that is roughly 1-foot in diameter when it is 1inch away from the screen, it will produce a slightly cooler, but larger basking spot when moved back another 6 inches or so.

Ceramic Heat Emitters
Ceramic heat emitters are small inserts that function similarly to light bulbs, except that they do not produce any visible light – they only produce heat.

Ceramic heat emitters are used in reflector-dome fixtures, just as heat lamps are. The benefits of such devices are numerous:

- They typically last much longer than light bulbs do

- They are suitable for use with thermostats

- They allow for the creation of overhead basking spots, as lights do

- They can be used day or night

However, the devices do have three primary drawbacks:

- They are very hot when in operation

- They are much more expensive than light bulbs

- You cannot tell by looking if they are hot or cool. This can be a safety hazard – touching a ceramic heat emitter while it is hot is likely to cause serious burns.

Radiant Heat Panels

Quality radiant heat panels are a great choice for heating most reptile habitats, including those containing basilisks. Radiant heat panels are essentially heat pads that stick to the roof of the habitat. They usually feature rugged, plastic or metal casings and internal reflectors to direct the infrared heat back into the cage.

Radiant heat panels have a number of benefits over traditional heat lamps and under tank heat pads:

- They do not produce visible light, which means they are useful for both diurnal and nocturnal heat production. They can be used in conjunction with fluorescent light fixtures during the day, and remain on at night once the lights go off.

- They are inherently flexible. Unlike many devices that do not work well with pulse-proportional thermostats, most radiant heat panels work well with on-off and pulse-proportional thermostats.

The only real drawback to radiant heat panels is their cost: radiant heat panels often cost about two to three times the price of light- or heat pad-oriented systems. However, many radiant heat panels outlast light bulbs and heat pads, a fact that offsets their high initial cost over the long term.

Heat Pads

Heat pads are useful for keeping the ambient cage temperatures warm, but they aren't ideal for creating a basking spot for basilisks.

Additionally, heating pads do have a few drawbacks:

- Heat pads have a high risk for causing contact burns.

- If they malfunction, they can damage the cage as well as the surface on which they are placed.

- They are probably more likely to cause a fire than heat lamps or radiant heat panels are.

However, if installed properly (which includes allowing fresh air to flow over the exposed side of the heat pad) and used in conjunction with a thermostat, they can be reasonably safe. With heat pads, it behooves the keeper to purchase premium products, despite the small increase in price.

Heat Tape

Heat tape is somewhat akin to a "stripped down" heat pad. In fact, most heat pads are simply pieces of heat tape that have already been connected and sealed inside a plastic envelope.

Heat tape is primarily used to heat large numbers of cages simultaneously. While it can be used in a manner similar to that in which heat pads are used, it is generally inappropriate for novices, and requires the keeper to make electrical connections. Additionally, a thermostat is always required when using heat tape.

Historically, heat tape was used to keep water pipes from freezing – not to heat reptile cages. While some commercial heat tapes have been designed specifically for reptiles, many have not. Accordingly, it may be illegal, not to mention dangerous, to use heat tapes for purposes other than for which they are designed.

Heat Cables

Heat cables are similar to heat tape, in that they heat a long strip of the cage, but they are much more flexible and easy to use. Like heat tape and heat pads, they are best used to control the cage's ambient temperatures, rather than to provide a basking spot. Many heat cables are suitable to use inside the cage, while others are designed for use outside the habitat.

Always be sure to purchase heat cables that are designed to be used in reptile cages. Those sold at hardware stores are not appropriate for use in a cage. Heat cables must be used in conjunction with a thermostat, or, at the very least, a rheostat.

Hot Rocks

In the early days of commercial reptile products, faux rocks, branches and caves with internal heating elements were very popular. However, they have generally fallen out of favor among modern keepers. These rocks and branches were often made with poor craftsmanship and cheap materials, causing them to fail and produce tragic results. Additionally, many keepers used the rocks improperly, leading to injuries, illnesses and death for many unfortunate reptiles.

Heated rocks are not designed to heat an entire cage; they are designed to provide a localized source of heat for the reptile. Nevertheless, many keepers tried to use them as the primary heat source for the cage, resulting in dangerously cool cage temperatures.

When lizards must rely on small, localized heat sources placed in otherwise chilly cages, they often hug these heat sources for extended periods of time. This can lead to serious thermal burns – whether or not the unit functions properly. This illustrates the key reason why these devices make adequate supplemental heat sources, but they should not be used as primary heating sources.

Modern hot rocks utilize better features, materials and craftsmanship than the old models did, but they still offer few benefits to the keeper or the kept. Additionally, any heating devices that are designed to be used inside the cage necessitate passing an electric cable through a hole, which is not always easy to accomplish. However, some cages do feature passageways for chords.

Nocturnal Temperatures

Basilisks are tropical animals whose habitat should not cool much at night. They do appreciate a slight drop in temperatures throughout the night, but in general, their cages shouldn't drop below the low 70s Fahrenheit (22 to 23 Celsius).

However, it is important to avoid using visible light to heat your basilisk's habitat at night, to avoid upsetting his day-night cycles. This is easily accomplished by using a heat pad, heat tape or heat cables to warm the cage at night – these devices create no visible light, and will not disturb your pet's activity. Alternatively, radiant heat panels, red light bulbs or ceramic heat emitters can also be used to provide the heat your lizard needs.

Thermometers

It is important to monitor the cage temperatures very carefully to ensure your pet stays health. Just as a water test kit is an aquarist's best friend, quality thermometers are some of the most important husbandry tools for reptile keepers.

Ambient and Surface Temperatures

Two different types of temperature are relevant for pet lizards: ambient temperatures and surface temperatures.

The ambient temperature in your animal's enclosure is the air temperature; the surface temperatures are the temperatures of the objects in the cage. Both are important to monitor, as they can differ widely.

Measure the cage's ambient temperatures with a digital thermometer. An indoor-outdoor model will feature a probe that allows you to measure the temperature at both ends of the thermal gradient at once. For example, you may position the thermometer at the cool side of the cage, but attach the remote probe to a branch near the basking spot.

Because standard digital thermometers do not measure surface temperatures well, use a non-contact, infrared thermometer for such measurements. These devices will allow you to measure surface temperatures accurately from a short distance away.

Thermal Control Equipment

Some heating devices, such as heat lamps, are designed to operate at full capacity for the entire time that they are turned on. Such devices should not be used with thermostats – instead, care should be taken to calibrate the proper temperature.

Other devices, such as heat pads, heat tape and radiant heat panels are designed to be used with a regulating device to maintain the proper temperature, such as a thermostat or rheostat.

Rheostats

Rheostats are similar to light-dimmer switches, and they allow you to reduce the output of a heating device. In this way, you can dial in the proper temperature for the habitat.

The drawback to rheostats is that they only regulate the amount of power going to the device – they do not monitor the cage temperature or adjust the power flow automatically. In practice, even with the same level of power entering the device, the amount of heat generated by most heat sources varies over the course of the day.

If you set the rheostat so that it keeps the cage at the right temperature in the morning, it may become too hot by the middle of the day. Conversely, setting the proper temperature during the middle of the day may leave the morning temperatures too cool.

Care must be taken to ensure that the rheostat controller is not inadvertently bumped or jostled, causing the temperature to rise or fall outside of healthy parameters.

Thermostats

Thermostats are similar to rheostats, except that they also feature a temperature probe that monitors the temperature in the cage (or under the basking source). This allows the thermostat to adjust the power going to the device as necessary to maintain a predetermined temperature.

For example, if you place the temperature probe under a basking spot powered by a radiant heat panel, the thermostat will keep the temperature relatively constant under the basking site.

There are two different types of thermostats: on-off thermostats and pulse proportional thermostats.

On-Off Thermostats
"On-Off" thermostats work by cutting the power to the device when the probe's temperature reaches a given temperature.

For example, if the thermostat were set to 85 degrees Fahrenheit (29 degrees Celsius), the heating device would turn off whenever the temperature exceeds this threshold. When the temperature falls below 85, the thermostat restores power to the unit, and the heater begins functioning again. This cycle will continue to repeat, thus maintaining the temperature within a relatively small range.

Be aware that on-off thermostats have a "lag" factor, meaning that they do not turn off when the temperature reaches a given temperature. They turn off when the temperature is a few degrees *above* that temperature, and then turn back on when the temperate is a little *below* the set point. Because of this, it is important to avoid setting the temperature at the limits of your pet's acceptable range. Some premium models have an adjustable amount of threshold for this factor, which is helpful.

Pulse Proportional Thermostats

Pulse proportional thermostats work by constantly sending pulses of electricity to the heater. By varying the rate of pulses, the amount of energy reaching the heating devices varies.

A small computer inside the thermostat adjusts this rate to match the set-point temperature as measured by the probe. Accordingly, pulse proportional thermostats maintain much more consistent temperatures than on-off thermostats do.

Lights should not be used with thermostats, as the constant flickering may stress your pet. Conversely, heat pads, heat tape, radiant heat panels and ceramic heat emitters should always be used with either a rheostat or, preferably, a thermostat to avoid overheating your basilisk.

Thermostat Failure

If used for long enough, all thermostats eventually fail. The question is will yours fail today or twenty years from now. While some thermostats fail in the "off" position, a thermostat that fails in the "on" position may overheat your lizard. Unfortunately, tales of entire collections being lost to a faulty thermostat are too common.

Accordingly, it behooves the keeper to acquire high-quality thermostats. Some keepers use two thermostats, connected in series arrangement. By setting the second thermostat (the "backup thermostat") a few degrees higher than the setting used on the "primary thermostat," you safeguard yourself against the failure of either unit.

In such a scenario, the backup thermostat allows the full power coming to it to travel through to the heating device, as the temperature never reaches its higher set-point temperature.

However, if the first unit fails in the "on" position, the second thermostat will keep the temperatures from rising too high. The temperature will rise a few degrees in accordance with the higher set-point temperature, but it will not get hot enough to harm your pet.

If the backup thermostat fails in the "on" position, the first thermostat retains control. If either fails in the "off" position, the temperature will fall until you rectify the situation, but a brief exposure to relatively cool temperatures is unlikely to be fatal.

Chapter 8: Lighting the Enclosure

Sunlight plays an important role in the lives of most diurnal lizards, including basilisks. It is always preferable to afford captive basilisks access to unfiltered sunlight, but this is not always possible. In these cases, it is necessary to provide your lizard with high quality lighting, which can partially satisfy their need for real sunlight.

Basilisks deprived of appropriate lighting may become seriously ill. Learning how to provide the proper lighting for reptiles is sometimes an arduous task for beginners, but it is very important to the long-term health of your pet that you do. To understand the type of light your lizard needs, you must first understand a little bit about light.

The Electromagnetic Spectrum

Light is a type of energy that physicists call electromagnetic radiation; it travels in waves. These waves may differ in amplitude, which correlates to the vertical distance between consecutive wave crests and troughs, frequency, which correlates with the number of crests per unit of time, and wavelength.

Wavelength is the distance from one crest to the next, or one trough to the next. Wavelength and frequency are inversely proportional, meaning that as the wavelength increases, the frequency decreases. It is more common for reptile keepers to discuss wavelengths rather than frequencies.

The sun produces energy (light) with a very wide range of constituent wavelengths. Some of these wavelengths fall within a range called the visible spectrum; humans can detect these rays with their eyes. Such waves have wavelengths between about 390 and 700 nanometers. Rays with wavelengths longer or shorter than these limits are broken into their own groups and given different names.

Those rays with around 390 nanometer wavelengths or less are called ultraviolet rays or UV rays. UV rays are broken down into three different categories, just as the different colors correspond with different wavelengths of visible light. UVA rays have wavelengths between 315 to 400 nanometers, while UVB rays have wavelengths between 280 and 315 nanometers while UVC rays have wavelengths between 100 and 280 nanometers.

Rays with wavelengths of less than 280 nanometers are called x-rays and gamma rays. At the other end of the spectrum, infrared rays have wavelengths longer than 700 nanometers; microwaves and radio waves are even longer.

UVA rays are important for food recognition, appetite, activity and eliciting natural behaviors. UVB rays are necessary for many reptiles to produce vitamin D3. Without this vitamin, reptiles cannot properly metabolize their calcium.

Light Color

The light that comes from the sun and light bulbs is composed of a combination of wavelengths, which create the blended white light that you perceive. This combination of wavelengths varies slightly from one light source to the next.

The sun produces very balanced white light, while "economy" incandescent bulbs produce relatively fewer blue rays and yields a yellow-looking light. High-quality bulbs designed for reptiles often produce very balanced, white light. The degree to which light causes objects to look as they would under sunlight is called the Color Rendering Index, or CRI. Sunlight has a CRI of 100, while quality bulbs have CRIs of 80 to 90; by contrast, a typical incandescent bulb has a CRI of 40 to 50

Light Brightness

Another important characteristic of light that relates to basilisks is luminosity, or the brightness of light. Measured in units called Lux, luminosity is an important consideration for your lighting system. While you cannot possibly replicate the intensity of the sun's light, it is desirable in most circumstances to ensure the habitat is lit as well as is reasonably possible.

For example, in the tropics, the sunlight intensity averages around 100,000 Lux at midday; by comparison, the lights in a typical family living room only produce about 50 Lux.

Without access to bright lighting, many reptiles become lethargic, depressed or exhibit hibernating behaviors. Dim lighting may inhibit feeding and cause lizards to become stressed and ill.

Nevertheless, it is important to remember that basilisks spend most of their lives living in the dappled light under the forest canopy. Accordingly, while it is important to provide very bright lighting in portions of the cage, you must also provide the lizards with shade, into which they can retreat if they desire.

Your Lizard's Lighting Needs

To reiterate, basilisks (and most other diurnal lizards) require:

- Light that is comprised of visible light, as well as UVA and UVB wavelengths

- Light with a high color-rendering index

- Light of the sufficiently strong intensity

Now that you know what your lizard requires, you can go about designing the lighting system for his habitat. Ultraviolet radiation is the most difficult component of proper lighting to provide, so it makes sense to begin by examining the types of bulbs that produce UV radiation.

The only commercially produced bulbs that produce significant amounts of UVA and UVB and suitable for a basilisk habitat are linear fluorescent light bulbs, compact fluorescent light bulbs and mercury vapor bulbs.

Neither type of fluorescent bulb produces significant amounts of heat, but mercury vapor bulbs produce a lot of heat and serve a dual function. In many cases, keepers elect to use both types of lights – a mercury vapor bulb for a warm basking site with high levels of UV radiation and fluorescent bulbs to light the rest of the cage without raising the temperature. You can also use fluorescent bulbs to provide the requisite UV radiation and use a regular incandescent bulb to generate the basking spot.

Fluorescent bulbs have a much longer history of use than mercury vapor bulbs, which makes some keepers more comfortable using them. However, many models only produce moderate amounts of UVB radiation. While some mercury vapor bulbs produce significant quantities of UVB, some question the wisdom of producing more UV radiation than the animal receives in the wild. Additionally, mercury vapor bulbs are much too powerful to use in small habitats, and they are more expensive initially.

Most fluorescent bulbs must be placed within 12 inches of the basking surface, while some mercury vapor bulbs should be placed farther away from the basking surface – be sure to read the manufacturer's instructions before use. Be sure that the bulbs you purchase specifically state the amount of UVB radiation they produce; this figure is expressed as a percentage, for example 7% UVB. Most UVB-producing bulbs require replacement every six to 12 months – whether or not they have stopped producing light.

However, ultraviolet radiation is only one of the characteristics that lizard keepers must consider. The light bulbs used must also produce a sunlight-like spectrum. Fortunately, most high-quality light bulbs that produce significant amounts of UVA and UVB radiation also feature a high color-rendering index. The higher the CRI, the better, but any bulbs with a CRI of 90 or above will work well. If you are having trouble deciding between two otherwise evenly matched bulbs, select the one with the higher CRI value.

Brightness is the final, and easiest, consideration for the keeper to address. While no one yet knows what the ideal luminosity for a basilisk's cage, it makes sense to ensure that part of the cage features very bright lighting. However, you should always offer a shaded retreat within the enclosure into which your lizard can avoid the light if he desires.

Connect the lights to an electric timer to keep the length of the day and night consistent. Basilisks thrive with 12 hours of daylight and 12 hours of darkness all year long.

Chapter 9: Substrate and Furniture

Once you have purchased or constructed your basilisk's enclosure, you must place appropriate items inside it. In general, these items take the form of an appropriate substrate and the proper cage furniture, which may include live plants, hiding locations and perches for climbing.

Substrate

Substrate is a contentious issue among lizard keepers. For every keeper touting a given substrate, there are two others who claim that it is a poor choice. In truth, there is no perfect substrate, so it is always a matter of making choices between the pros and cons of each.

Paper Products

Newspaper, paper towels and commercial cage liners are acceptable for use with basilisks, but they aren't ideal for long-term maintenance. Basilisks are active lizards, whose claws will quickly rip these substrates apart. The only real benefit paper substrates offer basilisk keepers is that they make it easier to clean the cage floor – you can simply remove the paper each day and replace it with a fresh sheet.

Paper substrates also give insects places to hide, so be sure to check underneath the paper periodically, and flush out any hiding insects.

Cypress Mulch

Cypress mulch is one of the most popular substrate choices for basilisk maintenance. It not only looks attractive, but it retains moisture and has a pleasant odor. It is often relatively inexpensive too.

One drawback to cypress mulch is that some brands (or individual bags among otherwise good brands) produce a stick-like mulch, rather than mulch composed of thicker pieces. These sharp sticks can injure the keeper and the kept. It usually only takes one cypress mulch splinter jammed under a keeper's fingernail to cause them to switch substrates.

Cypress mulch does not represent a very significant ingestion hazard, but fine fibers may be inadvertently consumed, with potentially dangerous results.

Cypress mulch is available from most home improvement and garden centers, as well as pet supply retailers. No matter the source you use, be sure that the product contains 100 percent cypress mulch without any demolition or salvage content.

Fir (Orchid) Bark

The bark of fir trees is often used for orchid propagation, and so it is often called "orchid bark." Orchid bark is very attractive, and, thanks to its relatively uniform shape, does not represent as much of an ingestion hazard as cypress mulch does.

Orchid bark is rather easy to spot clean, which helps to reduce the costs associated with its use. However, monthly replacement can be expensive for those living in the Eastern United States and Europe.

Soils

Soil is another acceptable substrate for basilisks. You can make a suitable soil substrate by digging up your own soil, purchasing organic soil products or mixing your own blend.

Avoid products containing perlite, manure, fertilizers, pre-emergent herbicides or other additives. Sterilization of the soil before adding it to the enclosure is not strictly necessary; in fact, many of the microorganisms present will help breakdown waste products from your lizard.

Substrate Comparison Chart

Substrate	Pros	Cons
Cypress Mulch	Absorbs and retains water and easy to spot clean.	Ingestion hazard. Messy.
Fir (Orchid) Bark	Absorbs and retains water, attractive and easy to spot clean.	Ingestion hazard. Messy. Provides hiding places for insects.
Newspaper	Absorbs and retains water, attractive and easy to spot clean.	Ingestion hazard. Messy. Provides hiding places for insects. Expensive.
Commercial Paper Products	Absorbs *some* water. Safe, low-cost. Easy to maintain.	Unattractive. Provides hiding places for insects.
Soil	Retains moisture. Safe, low-cost. Attractive.	Messy.

Substrates to Avoid

Some substrates are completely inappropriate for basilisk maintenance, and should be avoided at all costs. These include:

- **Cedar Shavings** – Cedar shavings produce toxic fumes that may sicken or kill your lizard. Always avoid cedar shavings.

- **Gravel** – You can use large gravel as a substrate, but its problems outweigh its benefits. Gravel must be washed when soiled, which is laborious and time consuming. Gravel is also quite heavy, which can cause headaches for the keeper.

- **Artificial Turf** – Although it seems like a viable option with a number of benefits, artificial turf is not a good substrate for basilisks. Keeping artificial turf clean is difficult, and the threads may come loose and wrap around your lizard's tail, tongue or toes.

Cage Furniture

To complete your basilisk's habitat, you must provide him with visual barriers to help keep his stress level low, and perches on which he can bask.

The easiest way to provide visual barriers for your lizard is by keeping live or fake plants in the enclosure and providing several hiding spaces, into which he can retreat when he likes.

Cork bark

The outer bark of the cork oak (*Quercus suber*), cork bark is available in both tubes and flat slabs. Either work well for basilisk maintenance, although flat slabs can be arranged to provide your lizard with snugger hiding places.

The primary downsides to cork bark relate to its price (it is often rather expensive) and its tendency to collect debris in the cracks on its surface, which makes cleaning difficult.

Cork bark is also works when used as climbing perches. You'll just need to figure out a way to place of affix it in a way that allows your basilisk to climb it.

Cardboard and Other Disposable Hides

Cardboard tubes, boxes or sheets also make excellent hiding spaces, as do sections of foam egg crate. These materials are light weight, very low cost and easy to replace once soiled.

Cardboard and similar items do not make very attractive hiding places, but this is only a human concern – your lizard will not mind at all.

Commercial Hides

There are a number of commercially produced hiding spaces that you can use for your basilisk. Some are made of wood, while others are made of plastic or ceramic. The latter two materials will last longer and are easier to clean, so they are generally preferable to wooden hiding spaces.

Unfortunately, many commercial hides are too large to serve their desired purpose – basilisks like to hide in small, tight places, rather than spacious voids. When possible, they prefer to feel the top of the hide against their back when inside – this makes them feel more secure.

Plastic Plant Saucers

By inverting a plastic plant saucer and cutting a "door" into one of the sides, you can make very effective and affordable hiding spots for your lizard. In fact, these saucers are so inexpensive that it usually makes sense to purchase a stack of them – this way you can place two or three in the enclosure for your lizard to use, while keeping a few others ready for easy replacement, when it comes time to wash the ones in use.

Be sure to use the opaque plant saucers, rather than the transparent ones, as these would defeat the entire purpose of a hiding space.

Plants

Plants are also valuable additions for a basilisk's cage. Most keepers opt to use silk or plastic plants in their enclosures. This is a good option, but you must observe your lizard closely to ensure he or she does not attempt to eat the fake plants.

It is possible to use live plants in your lizard's enclosure, but because you must ensure that the plants are not toxic to the animals and they survive in the enclosure, the options are relatively few.

Always wash all plants before placing them in the enclosure to help remove any pesticide residues. It is also wise to discard the potting soil used for the plant and replace it with fresh soil, which you know contains no pesticides, perlite or fertilizer.

While you can plant cage plants directly in soil substrates, this complicates maintenance and makes it difficult to replace the substrate regularly. Accordingly, it is generally preferable to keep the plant in some type of container.

Perches

Basilisks need at least one perch in their habitat, but it is usually wise to provide two or three in total. Try to strike a good balance between offering your pet plenty of perches, without overly crowding the habitat.

Basilisks are skilled climbers, but they prefer very broad, flat branches and logs, as opposed to the thin branches preferred by chameleons and other tree-climbers.

Many different types of branches can be used in basilisk cages. Most non-aromatic hardwoods suffice. See the chart at the end of the chapter for specific recommendations.

You can purchase climbing branches from pet and craft stores, or you can collect them yourself. Try to use branches that are still attached to trees (always obtain permission first). Such branches will harbor fewer insects and other invertebrate pests than dead branches will.

Always wash branches with plenty of hot water and a stiff, metal-bristled scrub brush to remove as much dirt, dust and fungus as possible before placing them in your basilisk's cage. Clean stubborn spots with a little bit of dish soap, but be sure to rinse them thoroughly afterwards.

Whether you purchased them from a pet store or collected them from the forest, it is advisable to sterilize all branches before placing them in a cage. The easiest way to do so is by placing the branch in a 300-degree oven for about 15 minutes. Doing so should kill most pests and pathogens lurking inside the wood.

You can often place branches diagonally across the enclosure, in such a way that alleviates the need for direct attachment to the cage. However, horizontal branches will require secure points of attachment so they do not fall and injure your pet.

You can attach the branches to the cage in a variety of different ways. Be sure to make it easy to remove the branches, so you can clean them as necessary.

You can use hooks and eye-screws to suspend branches, which allows for quick and easy removal, but it is only applicable for cages with walls that will accept and support the eye-screws. You can also make "closet rod holders" by cutting a slot into small PVC caps, which are attached to the cage frame.

Recommended Tree Species for Perches

Recommended Species	Species to Avoid
Maple trees (*Acer* spp.)	**Cherry trees** (*Prunus* spp.)
Oak trees (*Quercus* spp.)	**Pine trees** (*Pinus* spp.)
Walnut trees (*Juglans* spp.)	**Cedar trees** (*Cedrus* spp., etc.)
Ash trees (*Fraxinus* spp.)	**Juniper trees** (*Juniperus* spp.)
Dogwood trees (*Cornus* spp.)	**Poison ivy / oak** (*Toxicodendron* spp.)
Sweetgum trees (*Liquidambar stryaciflua*)	
Crepe Myrtle trees (*Lagerstroemia* spp.)	
Willow trees (*Salix* spp.)	
Tuliptrees (*Liriodendron tulipifera*)	
Pear trees (*Pyrus* spp.)	
Apple trees (*Malus* spp.)	
Manzanitas (*Arctostaphylos* spp.)	
Grapevine (*Vitis* spp.)	

Chapter 10: Providing Water to Your Basilisk

Like most other animals, basilisks require drinking water to remain healthy. However, the relative humidity (the amount of water in the air) is also an important factor in their health.

While drinking water helps to keep basilisks hydrated, the moisture in the air helps to keep their skin healthy and prevents respiratory problems from developing.

Providing Drinking Water

Providing ample drinking water is imperative to the health of your new pet. Fortunately, basilisks readily drink from a water dish, unlike some other lizards, who fail to recognize standing water for what it is.

Keep a shallow water dish in the habitat with your basilisk at all times. You can purchase a commercially made water dish, or you can use plastic plant saucers, storage boxes or cat litter pans. Because basilisks like to spend a lot of time in the water, and they require a high humidity to remain healthy, it is often beneficial to use a very large water dish whenever possible. Keeping a large water dish clean and full can be challenging, but that is simply one of the responsibilities that is inherent to basilisk maintenance.

Basilisks – particularly adults – are strong swimmers, but use care when providing the water dish. Be sure that they can easily enter and exit the dish before filling it with water.

Water Quality

Some keepers prefer to give their lizard dechlorinated or purified or spring water, but others simply offer tap water. Purified bottled water and spring water are typically safe for lizards, but distilled water should be avoided to prevent causing electrolyte imbalances.

It is wise to have tap water tested to ensure that heavy metals or other pollutants are not present before offering it to your basilisk.

Humidity

Basilisks are lizards of rainforests (actually, they are lizards of riparian areas within rainforests), so they require very high humidity in order to thrive. Accordingly, you should provide them with a moderately humid, yet adequately ventilated enclosure (wet, warm stagnant air will encourage the proliferation of bacteria and fungi).

You can keep the enclosure suitably humid through a combination of a large water dish, a moisture-retaining substrate (such as cypress mulch) and by misting the cage daily with clean, room-temperature water. When you mist the habitat, spray the walls, cage furniture and plants; if your lizard doesn't react negatively, you can even mist him gently.

Additionally, it is wise to provide them with a small hide that contains a bit of damp substrate or moss (this is in addition to at least one "dry" hide), which they may use prior to shed cycles.

Note that the type of cage you use will influence the humidity of your pet's habitat. Generally speaking, the more ventilation the cage has, the drier it will tend to be, as the enclosure will usually be warmer than the air in your home. This means that keepers using aquariums with screened lids must be sure to avoid allowing the cage to become too dry, while keepers using small plastic storage containers featuring only a dozen or so air holes, must guard against letting the habitat become too damp.

Chapter 11: Feeding Basilisks

Basilisks are omnivores, who primarily feed on invertebrates, small vertebrates and some plant material.

The best diet for captive basilisks is one that mimics their wild diet, being primarily comprised of gut-loaded insects, supplemented with the occasional pre-killed rodent and some soft fruits and vegetables. It is not strictly necessary to feed basilisks rodents or other vertebrate prey, and it is important to avoid providing too many rodents to your lizard, but rodents can make a nutritious component of a basilisk's diet.

Like most other species, basilisks benefit from a varied diet, which helps to minimize the effects of dietary excess and vitamin and mineral deficiencies. However, providing a varied diet is not always sufficient to avoid deficiencies, so it is wise to supplement some of your pet's food with additional vitamins and minerals. Discuss a proper dosing regimen and schedule with your veterinarian.

Insects

Insects should form the bulk of the diet for basilisks of all sizes. Crickets or roaches make a nice staple, while the other insects can be incorporated to add variety.

Some keepers supplement their pet's diet with wild caught insects, but discretion is advised, as such insects may be contaminated with pesticides or infested with parasites.

The following insects make suitable prey for basilisks:

- Crickets

- Roaches

- Mealworms

- Giant mealworms

- Superworms

- Wax worms

- Grasshoppers

Other Invertebrates

Aside from insects, a number of invertebrates make suitable food sources for basilisks. However, few are available commercially, so they rarely form more than a trivial portion of a captive lizard's diet.

A few examples of acceptable invertebrates include:

- Earthworms

- Snails

- Slugs

- Roly polies

Vertebrates

In the wild, large basilisks occasionally consume small lizards, fish, frogs and snakes. While your lizard will remain perfectly healthy without eating any vertebrate prey, it is acceptable to offer the occasional vertebrate to your pet. However, some vertebrates present a few additional challenges to the keeper.

Rodents are the most prudent vertebrate prey item to feed to your basilisk, because they rarely contain parasites that will infect your lizard and they are widely available in the marketplace. Newborn ("pink") or furred ("furry") mice are the best size for most lizards, although very large basilisks can probably handle weaned ("hopper") mice without much trouble.

If you choose to offer rodents to your pet, offer pre-killed, rather than live, individuals, to avoid any suffering on the part of the rodent. Live newborn rodents will not harm your lizard, but weaned rodents may be able to inflict a painful bite in self-defense. Nevertheless, it is important to treat all feeder animals with respect and avoid any unnecessary suffering.

Neither lizards nor snakes nor frogs should not be offered as prey, as they are likely to be infested with parasites, which they may transmit to your pet. Small captive bred (and presumably parasite-free) lizards or snakes would theoretically be acceptable, but are not likely to be cost effective.

A plumed basilisk consuming an earthworm.

Minnows and goldfish present similar problems, although it may be possible to set up a small breeding tank, so that you can produce your own. You'll need to first establish a parasite-free colony with the help of a veterinarian, but then (assuming sound husbandry practices) the offspring should be parasite free, and therefore suitable food for your basilisk.

Prey Size

Mature basilisks can easily handle and consume relatively large insects; adult crickets and large roaches are rarely a problem.

Juveniles, by contrast, are much too small to consume large insects. In fact, feeding large insects to small basilisks can cause them to become impacted. In some cases, this can be fatal. To avoid such eventualities, offer small lizards insects that are no longer than the distance between the lizard's eyes.

How to Offer Food

Keepers can offer prey in a few different ways. If the cage is suitably secure, you can just release a few insects into the cage at a time. Use care to avoid releasing too many feeder insects into the cage at a time, as some of the insects may hide and large numbers of free-roaming insects may stress or injure your pet.

Alternatively, you can offer insects individually by hand or via forceps. Hand feeding is laborious, but acceptable if you do not mind devoting this amount of time to your pet's daily feedings. You can also use a feeding cup, which will keep the insects contained until the lizard eats them.

If you elect to use a feeding cup, you will need to select a cup that is tall enough to keep the insects contained, and yet short enough that the lizard can reach them.

You can allow insects to sit in the feeding cup for about 24 hours, but do not let them sit in here for any longer. Clean the feeding cup daily with soap and water, and disinfect it periodically.

Feeding Quantity and Frequency

Offer mature basilisks food every day or every other day. Provide your pet with as many insects as he will eat in about 10 minutes.

Young basilisks will benefit from slightly smaller, yet more frequent meals. Accordingly, feed young lizards as many insects as they will eat in 2 or 3 minutes, but provide them with two or three daily meals.

Always remove any uneaten insects after the allotted time to prevent them from harming your pet.

Fruits and Vegetables

Although basilisks primarily subsist on animal-based foods, vegetation also plays an important role in their diet. In addition to being rich in vitamins and minerals, most plant material is full of water, which will help keep your lizard hydrated.

While some lizards will consume a variety of leafy green vegetables, basilisks usually prefer soft fruits and flowers. Typically, adults demonstrate more interest in plant matter than juveniles do, but you can certainly offer plant materials to young basilisks.

Here are a few foods that you can offer to your basilisk. Remember that your lizard is an individual, with his own unique preferences and favorites – he may like some and avoid others.

- Dandelions
- Hibiscus
- Roses
- Cilantro
- Parsley
- Carrots
- Squash
- Zucchini
- Pumpkin
- Kiwi
- Peaches

- Strawberries
- Blueberries
- Blackberries

Always wash all fruits and vegetables before offering them to your pet, to help remove any waxes or pesticides. Remove and replace the leaf after about 24 hours to prevent it from spoiling.

A twice-weekly offering of plant material is likely sufficient for your pet's health, but there is little downside to offering plant material more often than this, if your pet is interested. Young basilisks may show less interest in plant matter than adults do, but continue to offer them to your pet to instill good eating habits.

Vitamin and Mineral Supplements

Many keepers add commercially produced vitamin and mineral supplements to their basilisk's food on a regular basis. In theory, these supplements help to correct dietary deficiencies and ensure that captive lizards get a balanced diet. In practice, things are not this simple.

While some vitamins and minerals are unlikely to build up to toxic levels, others may very well cause problems if provided in excess. This means that you cannot simply apply supplements to every meal – you must decide upon a sensible supplementation schedule.

Additionally, it can be difficult to ascertain exactly how much of the various vitamins and minerals you will be providing to your lizard, as most such products are sold as fine powders, designed to be sprinkled on feeder insects. This is hardly a precise way to provide the proper dose to your lizard, and the potential for grossly over- or under-estimating the amount of supplement delivered is very real.

Because the age, sex and health of your basilisk all influence the amount of vitamins and minerals your pet requires, and each individual product has a unique composition, it is wise to consult your veterinarian before deciding upon a supplementation schedule. However, most keepers provide vitamin supplementation once each week, and calcium supplementation several times per week.

Chapter 12: Maintaining the Captive Habitat

Now that you have acquired your lizard and set up the enclosure, you must develop a protocol for maintaining his habitat. While basilisk habitats require major maintenance every month or so, they only require minor daily maintenance.

In addition to designing a husbandry protocol, you must embrace a record-keeping system to track your lizard's growth and health.

Cleaning and Maintenance Procedures

Once you have decided on the proper enclosure for your pet, you must keep your lizard fed, hydrated and ensure that the habitat stays in proper working order to keep your captive healthy and comfortable.

Some tasks must be completed each day, while others are should be performed weekly, monthly or annually.

Daily

- Monitor the ambient and surface temperatures of the habitat.

- Verify that your lizard has drinking water and mist the cage.

- Spot clean the cage to remove any loose insects, feces, urates or pieces of shed skin.

- Ensure that the lights, latches and other moving parts are in working order.

- Verify that your lizard is acting normally and appears healthy. You do not necessarily need to handle him to do so.

- Feed your lizard (some keepers only feed their captives four or five times per week).

- Ensure that the humidity and ventilation are at appropriate levels.

Weekly

- Change sheet-like substrates (newspaper, paper towels, etc.).

- Clean the inside surfaces of the enclosure.
- Inspect your lizard closely for any signs of injury, parasites or illness.

- Wash and sterilize all food dishes.

Monthly
- Break down the cage completely, remove and discard particulate substrates.

- Sterilize water containers and similar equipment in a mild bleach solution.

- Measure and weigh your lizard.

- Photograph your pet (recommended, but not imperative).

- Prune any plants as necessary.

Annually
- Replace the batteries in your thermometers and any other devices that use them.

- Replace any full-spectrum bulbs in use (some may require replacement every 6 months).

Cleaning your lizard's cage and furniture is relatively simple. Regardless of the way it became soiled, the basic process remains the same:

1. Rinse the object

2. Using a scrub brush or sponge and soapy water, remove any organic debris from the object.

3. Rinse the object thoroughly.

4. Disinfect the object.

5. Re-rinse the object.

6. Dry the object.

Chemicals & Tools
A variety of chemicals and tools are necessary for reptile care. Save yourself some time by purchasing dedicated cleaning products and keeping them in the same place that you keep your tools.

Spray Bottles

Misting your basilisk and his habitat with fresh water is one of the best ways to keep the cage humidity high. You can do this with a small, handheld misting bottle or a larger, pressurized unit (such as those used to spray herbicides). Automated units are available, but they are rarely cost-effective unless you are caring for a large colony of basilisks.

Scrub Brushes or Sponges

It helps to have a few different types of scrub brushes and sponges on hand for scrubbing and cleaning different items. Use the least abrasive sponge or brush suitable for the task to prevent wearing out cage items prematurely. Do not use abrasive materials on glass or acrylic surfaces. Steel-bristled brushes work well for scrubbing coarse, wooden items, such as branches.

Spatulas and Putty Knives

Spatulas, putty knives and similar tools are often helpful for cleaning reptile cages. For example, urates (which are not soluble in anything short of hot lava) often become stuck on cage walls or furniture. Instead of trying to dissolve them with harsh chemicals, just scrape them away with a sturdy plastic putty knife.

Spatulas and putty knives can also be helpful for removing wet newspaper, which often becomes stuck to the floor of the cage.

Small Vacuums

Small, handheld vacuums are very helpful for sucking up the dust left behind from substrates. They are also helpful for cleaning the cracks and crevices around the cage doors. A shop vacuum, with suitable hoses and attachments, can also be helpful, if you have enough room to store it.

Steam Cleaners

Steam cleaners are very effective for sterilizing cages, water bowls and durable cage props after they have been cleaned. In fact, steam is often a better choice than chemical disinfectants, as it will not leave behind a toxic residue. Never use a steam cleaner near your lizard, the plants in his cage or any other living organisms.

Soap

Use a gentle, non-scented dish soap. Antibacterial soap is preferred, but not necessary. Most people use far more soap than is necessary – a few drops mixed with a quantity of water is usually sufficient to help remove surface pollutants.

Bleach

Bleach (diluted to one-half cup per gallon of water) makes an excellent disinfectant. Be careful not to spill any on clothing, carpets or furniture, as it is likely to discolor the objects.

Always be sure to rinse objects thoroughly after using bleach and be sure that you cannot detect any residual odor. Bleach does not work as a disinfectant when in contact with organic substances; accordingly, items must be cleaned before you can disinfect them.

Veterinarian Approved Disinfectant

Many commercial products are available that are designed to be safe for their pets. Consult with your veterinarian about the best product for your situation, its method of use and its proper dilution.

Avoid Phenols

Always avoid cleaners that contain phenols, as they are extremely toxic to some reptiles. In general, do not use household cleaning products to avoid exposing your pet to toxic chemicals.

Keeping Records

It is important to keep records regarding your pet's health, growth and feeding, as well as any other important details. In the past, reptile keepers would do so on small index cards or in a notebook. In the modern world, technological solutions may be easier. For example, you can use your computer or mobile device to keep track of the pertinent info about your pet.

You can record as much information about your pet as you like, and the more information to you record, the better. But minimally, you should record the following:

Pedigree and Origin Information

Be sure to record the source of your lizard, the date on which you acquired him and any other data that is available. Breeders will often provide customers with information regarding the sire, dam, date of birth, weights and feeding records, but other sources will rarely offer comparable data.

Feeding Information

Record the date of each feeding, as well as the type of food item(s) offered. It is also helpful to record any preferences you may observe or any meals that are refused.

It is also wise to record the times you supplement the food with calcium or vitamin powders, unless you employ a standard weekly protocol.

Weights and Length

Because you look at your pet frequently, it is difficult to appreciate how quickly he is (or isn't) growing. Accordingly, it is important to track his size diligently.

Weigh your basilisk with a high quality digital scale. The scale must be sensitive to one-gram increments to be useful for very small lizards.

It is often easiest to use a dedicated "weighing container" with a known weight to measure your lizard. This way, you will not have to keep your pet stationary on the scale's platform – you can simply place him in the container and place the entire container on the scale. Subtract the weight of the container to obtain the weight of your lizard.

You can measure your lizard's length as well, but it is not as important as tracking his weight. It's often easier to measure his snout-vent length, rather than trying to include the tail in the measurement.

One easy way to get an approximation of your basilisks length is to place him in a clear-bottomed container, alongside a ruler. Lift the container above your head and look through the bottom of the container to compare your lizard's length against the ruler.

Maintenance Information

Record all of the noteworthy events associated with your pet's care. While it is not necessary to note that you misted the cage each day, it is appropriate to record the dates on which you changed the substrate or sterilized the cage.

Whenever you purchase new equipment, supplies or caging, note the date and source. This not only helps to remind you when you purchased the items, but it may help you track down a source for the items in the future, if necessary.

Breeding Information

If you intend to breed your lizard, you should record all details associated with pre-breeding conditioning, cycling, introductions, matings, color changes, copulations and egg deposition.

Record all pertinent information about any resulting clutches as well, including the number of viable eggs, as well as the number of unhatched and unfertilized eggs (often called "slugs" by reptile keepers).

Additionally, if you keep several lizards together in the same enclosure, you'll want to be careful to document the details of egg deposition, so you can be sure you know the correct parentage of each egg.

Record Keeping Samples

The following are two different examples of suitable recording systems.

The first example is reminiscent of the style employed by many with large collections. Because such keepers often have numerous animals, the notes are very simple, and require a minimum amount of writing or typing.

The second example demonstrates a simple approach that is employed by many with small collections (or a single pet): keeping notes on paper. Such notes could be taken in a notebook or journal, or you could type directly into a word processor. It does not matter *how* you keep records, just that you *do* keep records.

ID Number:	44522	Genus: Species/Sub:	Basiliscus plumifrons	Gender: DOB:	Male 3/20/16	CARD #2
6.30.15 Crickets	7.03.15 Crickets	7.08.15 Mealworms	7.14.15 Crickets	7.17.15 Mealworms		
7.01.15 Crickets	7.05.15 Crickets	7.09.15 Roaches	7.15.15 Shed	7.19.15 Roaches		
7.02.15 Mealworms	7.06.15 Crickets	7.12.15 Crickets	7.16.15 Crickets			

Date	Notes
4-22-13	Acquired "Dino" the plumed basilisk from a lizard breeder named Mark at the in-town reptile expo. Mark explained that Roger's scientific name is Basiliscus plumifrons. Cost was $150. Mark said he purchased the lizard in March, but he does not know the exact date.
4-23-13	Dino spent the night in the container I bought him in. I purchased a big plastic storage box, a heat lamp and a thermometer at the hardware store, and I ordered a non-contact thermometer online. I added an inverted plant saucer I bought at the hardware store for a hiding box, and a right-side-up saucer for the water dish.
4-27-13	Dino was really hungry! He ate 6 crickets in about 10 minutes.
4-30-13	I fed Dino 12 crickets and a mealworm today. He is so cute when he is trying to catch them!
5-1-13	Since Dino needs variety, I fed him a few roaches today. He seems to love roaches more than crickets, although mealworms seem to be his favorite.
5-3-13	Fed Dino a dozen crickets and a moth that flew into the house. He ate everything and looked like he wanted more.

Chapter 13: Interacting with Your Basilisk

Basilisks are not ideally suited for a great deal of hands-on contact. They are typically skittish and flighty lizards, who tend to view humans as dangerous predators. Most will flee at top speed when their keeper opens the habitat door and squirm incessantly once in the hand. Some may even result to biting, once grasped.

However, with proper technique and the right attitude, you can learn to handle your basilisk when the need arises. Your new pet may never be a "lap lizard," but, over time, he may become less nervous about your presence.

Handling a Basilisk

The very best way to handle your basilisk is to allow him to walk on your outstretched hands and forearms, rather than physically restraining him. However, few will behave in a manner conducive to this type of handling. You will usually need to grip these lizards gently but tightly, if you need to examine them closely or move them to a different location.

To pick up a very calm basilisk, you can try to slide a finger or two underneath the lizard's chin. Gently apply upward pressure, and the lizard will usually begin moving up your hand or finger. Keep lifting up gently and the lizard will likely crawl right into your hand voluntarily.

You can allow calm basilisks to walk around on your hand for 5 or 10 minutes, provided that the lizard does not begin showing signs of stress. Always be patient when transferring a basilisk to or from your hands. Try to "encourage" rather than "force" movements. Just be sure that you are ready for him to bolt at high speed.

While some lizards may hang out on your hand or arm while you tend to other duties, basilisks rarely will. Accordingly, it is wise to place him in a temporary holding cage while carry out cage maintenance or other tasks.

If your lizard will not crawl calmly around on your hands or arms (and most will not), then you'll need to gently but firmly grasp him around the body. Try to let his legs protrude through your fingers, which will be more comfortable for him, and provide some extra security.

Be aware that many basilisks will thrash about wildly when held and generally regard the encounter negatively. They may scratch with their legs, so some keepers like to wear gloves during the process. Basilisks can reach behind their back to deliver a bite, so try to keep your hands out of biting range.

Never grasp a basilisk by its tail.

In the Event of a Bite

While basilisks are not terribly inclined to bite, many will do so if sufficiently frightened. This may take little more than their keeper holding them; so, you should be prepared for the possibility, and understand the best course of action to take.

In the event of a basilisk bite, try to remain calm. Usually a frightened (or mistaken – do your fingers smell like crickets?) basilisk will release its bite fairly quickly. If he does not release his bite quickly, you can simply move him into his habitat, and place his feet on the ground – he'll usually let go once he feels that he can escape. If that doesn't work, you can try placing your hand under some cool, running water, which will normally cause him to let go.

Wash all bites with soap and warm water, and consult your doctor if the bite breaks the skin.

Transporting Your Pet

Although you should strive to avoid any unnecessary travel with your basilisk, circumstances often demand that you do (such as when your lizard becomes ill).

Strive to make the journey as stress-free as possible for your pet. This means protecting him from physical harm, as well as blocking as much stressful stimuli as possible.

The best type of container to use when transporting your basilisk is a plastic storage box. Add several ventilation holes to plastic containers to provide suitable ventilation. Place a few paper towels or some clean newspaper in the bottom of the box to absorb any fluids, should your lizard defecate or discharge urates during the journey.

Monitor your lizard regularly, but avoid constantly opening the container to take a peak. Checking up on your pet once every half-hour or so is more than sufficient.

Pay special attention to the enclosure temperatures while traveling. Use your digital thermometer to monitor the air temperatures inside the transportation container. Try to keep the temperatures in the high-70s Fahrenheit (24 to 26 degrees Celsius) so that your pet will remain comfortable. Use the air-conditioning or heater in your vehicle as needed to keep the animal within this range.

Keep your basilisk's transportation container as stable as possible while traveling. Do not jostle your pet unnecessarily and always use a gentle touch when moving the container. Never leave the container unattended.

Because you cannot control the thermal environment, it is not wise to take your lizard with you on public transportation.

Hygiene

Reptiles can carry *Salmonella* spp., *Escherichia coli* and several other zoonotic pathogens. Accordingly, it is imperative that you use good hygiene practices when handling reptiles.

Always wash your hands with soap and warm water each time you touch your pet, his habitat or the tools you use to care for him. Antibacterial soaps are preferred, but standard hand soap will suffice.

In addition to keeping your hands clean, you must also take steps to ensure your environment does not become contaminated with pathogens. In general, this means keeping your lizard and any of the tools and equipment you use to maintain his habitat separated from your belongings.

Establish a safe place for preparing his food, storing equipment and cleaning his habitat. Make sure these places are far from the places in which you prepare your food and personal effects. Never wash cages or tools in kitchens or bathrooms that are used by humans.

Always clean and sterilize any items that become contaminated by the germs from your lizard or his habitat.

Chapter 14: Common Health Concerns

Your basilisk cannot tell you when he is sick; like most other reptiles, these lizards endure illness stoically. This does not mean that injuries and illnesses do not cause them distress, but without expressive facial features, they do not *look* like they are suffering.

In fact, reptiles typically do not display symptoms until the disease has already reached an advanced state. Accordingly, it is important to treat injuries and illnesses promptly – often with the help of a qualified veterinarian –in order to provide your pet with the best chance of recovery.

Finding a Suitable Veterinarian

Basilisk keepers often find that it is more difficult to find a veterinarian to treat their lizard than it is to find a vet to treat a cat or dog. Relatively few veterinarians treat reptiles, so it is important to find a reptile-oriented vet *before* you need one. There are a number of ways to do this:

- You can search veterinarian databases to find one that is local and treats reptiles.

- You can inquire with your dog or cat vet to see if he or she knows a qualified reptile-oriented veterinarian to whom he or she can refer you.

- You can contact a local reptile-enthusiast group or club. Most such organizations will be familiar with the local veterinarians.

- You can inquire with local nature preserves or zoos. Most will have relationships with veterinarians that treat reptiles and other exotic animals.

Those living in major metropolitan areas may find a vet reasonably close, but rural reptile keepers may have to travel considerable distances to find veterinary assistance.

If you do not have a reptile-oriented veterinarian within driving distance, you can try to find a conventional veterinarian who is willing to consult with a reptile-oriented veterinarian via the phone or internet. These types of "two-for-one" visits may be expensive, as you will have to pay for both the actual visit and the consultation, but they may be your only option.

Reasons to Visit the Veterinarian

While reptiles do not require vaccinations or similar routine treatments, they may require visits to treat illnesses or injuries. However, you needn't travel to the vet every time your basilisk refuses a meal or experiences a bad shed. In fact, unnecessary veterinary visits may prove more harmful than helpful, so it is important to distinguish between those ailments that require care and those that are best treated at home.

When in doubt, contact your veterinarian and solicit his or her advice before packing up your lizard and hauling him in for an office visit. However, any of the following signs or symptoms can indicate serious problems, and each requires veterinary evaluation.

Visit your veterinarian when:

- Anytime your lizard wheezes, exhibits labored breathing or produces a mucus discharge from its nostrils or mouth.

- Your lizard produces soft or watery feces for longer than 48 hours.

- He suffers any significant injury. Common examples include thermal burns, friction damage to the rostral (nose) region or injured feet.

- Reproductive issues occur, such as being unable to deliver eggs. If a lizard appears nervous, agitated or otherwise stressed and unable to expel eggs, see your veterinarian immediately.

- Your lizard fails to feed for an extended period (more than three or four days).

- Your lizard displays any unusual lumps, bumps or lesions.

- Your lizard's intestines prolapse.

Ultimately, you must make all the decisions on behalf of your lizard, so weigh the pros and cons of each veterinary trip carefully and make the best decision you can for your pet. Just be sure that you always strive to act in his best interest.

Common Health Problems

The following are a few of the most common health problems that afflict basilisks. Their causes and the suggested course of action are also discussed.

Retained or Poor Sheds

Basilisks do not shed their entire skin at one time, as snakes do. Instead, they tend to shed in numerous pieces, over several hours or days. Occasionally, this can cause them to retain portions of their old skin. While this is not usually a big problem, care must be taken to ensure that the face, tail tip and toes all shed completely. If skin is retained in these places, blood flow can be restricted, eventually causing the death of the associated tissues. Sometimes this leads to the loss of toes or tail tips.

The best way to remove retained sheds is by temporarily increasing the enclosure humidity and misting your animal more frequently. In cases involving small amounts of retained skin, this may be enough to resolve the problem within a few days.

If this does not work, you may need to remove the retained skin manually. If the skin is partially free, you can try to get a grip on the loose part and gently pull the remaining skin free (do not try this if the retained skin attaches near the eyes).

If the retained skin is not peeling up around the edges, you will not be able to grip it. In such cases, use a damp paper towel to gently rub the area in question. With a little bit of water and gentle friction, you can usually dislodge the retained skin.

Always avoid forcing the skin off, as you may injure your pet. If the skin does not come off easily, return him to his cage and try again in 12 to 24 hours. Usually, repeated dampening will loosen the skin sufficiently to be removed.

If repeated treatments do not yield results, consult your veterinarian. He may feel that the retained shed is not causing a problem, and advise you to leave it attached – it should come off with the next shed. Alternatively, it if is causing a problem, the veterinarian can remove it without much risk of harming your pet.

Respiratory Infections

Like humans, lizards can suffer from respiratory infections. Basilisks with respiratory infections exhibit fluid or mucus draining from their nose and/or mouth, may be lethargic and are unlikely to eat. They may also spend excessive amounts of time basking on or under the heat source, in an effort to induce a "behavioral fever."

Bacteria, or, less frequently, fungi or parasites often cause respiratory infections. In addition, cleaning products, perfumes, pet dander and other particulate matter can irritate a reptile's respiratory tract as well. Some such bacteria and most fungi are ubiquitous, and only become problematic when they overwhelm an animal's immune system. Other bacteria and most viruses are transmitted from one lizard to another.

To reduce the chances of illnesses, keep your lizard separated from other lizards, keep his enclosure exceptionally clean and be sure to provide the best husbandry possible, in terms of temperature, ventilation and humidity. Additionally, avoid stressing your pet by handling him too frequently, or exposing him to chaotic situations.

Veterinary care is almost always required to treat respiratory infections. Your vet will likely take samples of the mucus and have it analyzed to determine the causal agent. The veterinarian will then prescribe medications, if appropriate, such as antibiotics.

It is imperative to carry out the actions prescribed by your veterinarian exactly as stated, and keep your lizard's stress level very low while he is healing. Stress can reduce immune function, so avoid handling him unnecessarily, and consider covering the front of his cage while he recovers.

"Mouth Rot"
Mouth rot – properly called stomatitis – is identified by noting discoloration, discharge or cheesy-looking material in your basilisk's mouth. Mouth rot can be a serious illness, and requires the attention of your veterinarian.

While mouth rot can follow an injury (such as happens when a lizard rubs his snout against the sides of the cage) it can also arise from systemic illness. Your veterinarian will cleanse your lizard's mouth and potentially prescribe an antibiotic.

Your veterinarian may recommend withholding food until the problem is remedied. Always be sure that lizards recovering from mouth rot have immaculately clean habitats, with appropriate temperature, humidity and ventilation, as well as ideal temperatures.

Internal Parasites
In the wild, most lizards carry some internal parasites. While it may not be possible to keep a reptile completely free of internal parasites, it is important to keep these levels in check.

Consider any wild-caught animals to be parasitized until proven otherwise. While most captive bred basilisks should have relatively few internal parasites, they are not immune to them.

Preventing parasites from building to pathogenic levels requires strict hygiene. Many parasites build up to dangerous levels when lizards are kept in cages that are continuously contaminated from feces.

Most internal parasites that are of importance for lizards are transmitted via the fecal-oral route. This means that eggs (or a similar life stage) of the parasites are released with the feces. If the lizard inadvertently ingests these, the parasites can develop inside his body and cause increased problems.

Parasite eggs are usually microscopic and easily carried by gentle drafts, where they may stick to cage walls or land in the feeding dish. Later, when the lizard snaps up an insect, he ingests the eggs as well.

Internal parasites may cause your lizard to vomit, pass loose stools, fail to grow or refuse food entirely. Other parasites may produce no obvious symptoms at all, despite causing considerable damage to your pet's internal organs. This illustrates the importance of routine fecal examinations (which do not necessarily require that you bring your pet into the office).

Your veterinarian will usually examine your pet's feces if he suspects internal parasites. By looking at the type of eggs inside the feces, your veterinarian can prescribe an appropriate medication. Many parasites are easily treated with anti-parasitic medications, but often, these medications must be given several times to eradicate the pathogens completely.

Some parasites may be transmissible to people, so always take proper precautions, including regular hand washing and keeping reptiles and their cages away from kitchens and other areas where foods are prepared.

Examples of common internal parasites include roundworms, tapeworms and amoebas.

External Parasites
Basilisks can theoretically suffer from external parasites, such as ticks and mites, but this appears to be a relatively rare occurrence.

Ticks should be removed manually. Using tweezers grasp the tick as close as possible to the lizard's skin and pull with steady, gentle pressure. Do not place anything over the tick first, such as petroleum jelly, or carry out any other "home remedies," such as burning the tick with a match. Such techniques may cause the tick to inject more saliva (which may contain diseases or bacteria) into the basilisk's body.

Drop the tick in a jar of isopropyl alcohol to kill it. It is a good idea to bring these to your veterinarian for analysis. Do not contact ticks with your bare hands, as many species can transmit disease to humans.

Mites are another matter entirely. While ticks are generally large enough to see easily, mites are about the size of a pepper flake. Whereas tick infestations usually only tally a few individuals, mite infestations may include thousands of individual parasites.

Mites may afflict wild caught lizards, but, as they are not confined to a small cage, such infestations are usually self-limiting. However, in captivity, mite infestations can approach plague proportions.

After a female mite feeds on a lizard, she drops off and finds a safe place (such as a tiny crack in a cage or among the substrate) to deposit her eggs. After the eggs hatch, they travel back to your pet (or to other lizards in your collection) where they feed and perpetuate the lifecycle.

Whereas a few mites may represent little more than an inconvenience to the lizard, significant infestations stress them considerably, and may even cause death through anemia. This is particularly true for small or young animals. Additionally, mites may transmit disease from one animal to another.

There are a number of different methods for eradicating a mite infestation. In each case, there are two primary steps that must be taken: You must eradicate the lizard's parasites as well as the parasites in the environment (which includes the room in which the cage resides).

Soaking is often a strategy for ridding a lizard of mites, but chemical treatments are occasionally necessary, instead. Consult with your veterinarian, who can recommend a prudent treatment.

You will also need to perform a thorough cage cleaning to eliminate the problem. To do so, you must remove everything from the cage, including water dishes, substrates and cage props. Sterilize all impermeable cage items, and discard the substrate and all porous cage props – including plants and trees. Vacuum the area around the cage and wipe down all of the nearby surfaces with a wet cloth.

It may be necessary to repeat this process several times to eradicate the mites completely. Accordingly, the very best strategy is to avoid contracting mites in the first place. This is why it is important to purchase your basilisk from a reliable breeder or retailer, and keep him quarantined from potential mite vectors.

Long-Term Anorexia

While basilisks may refuse the occasional meal, they should not fast for prolonged periods of time.

The most common reasons that lizards refuse food are improper temperatures and illness. Parasites and bacterial infections can also cause lizards to refuse food. Consult your veterinarian anytime that your pet refuses food for longer than three or four days.

Chapter 15: Breeding Basilisks

Basilisks are not bred with great regularity, but hobbyists and professional breeders do produce a small number of them each year. You can certainly accomplish the same, provided that you start with healthy animals and undertake the steps that have generally proven beneficial.

Sexing Basilisks

Obviously, you must have at least one sexual pair of animals to hope for viable eggs and eventual offspring. Fortunately, the sex of mature basilisks is relatively easy to discern. Juveniles, by contrast, are more difficult to identify as male or female.

Mature male basilisks can be distinguished from mature females by noting their large dorsal crests, which often extend down the back. Those of females are generally smaller, and limited to the head. However, there is some variation in crest size among the four species, so some subjective judgement is required.

Males also have a pair of bulges, visible on the ventral side of their tail base. This is created by the lizard's hemipenes, which are held inside the tail base when not in use. Females obviously lack hemipenes, and the associated bulges.

Some experienced keepers are able to identify the sex of sub-mature basilisks, but novice keepers often struggle to appreciate the fine differences displayed by young males and females.

Pre-Breeding Conditioning

Breeding reptiles always entails risk, so it is wise to refrain from breeding any animals that are not in excellent health. Breeding is especially stressful for female basilisks, who must withstand potential injuries during mating, and produce numerous, nutrient-rich eggs.

Animals slated for breeding trials must have excellent body weight, but obesity is to be avoided, as it is associated with reproductive problems. Ensure that the lizards are appropriately hydrated, and are free of parasites, infections and injuries.

Cycling

Cycling is the terms used to describe the climactic changes keepers impose upon their animals, which seek to mimic the natural seasonal changes in an animal's natural habitat.

For example, keepers may simulate winter conditions by reducing the enclosure temperatures and providing fewer hours of lighting. These changes are often necessary to stimulate captive reptiles into producing eggs, sperm or both. Alternatively, the humidity level of the enclosure can be manipulated to mimic a wet-season-dry-season pattern. This is typically the method used to induce breeding in basilisks. A dry season is used to "prime" the lizards for breeding, and a month or two later, a rainy season is initiated through copious misting of the habitat, which often stimulates the lizards to breed.

However, cycling is not always necessary for successful reproduction. Male and female basilisks may exhibit breeding behaviors anytime the temperatures are warm and the photoperiod is 12-hours-long or longer.

Care of the Gravid Female

Most breeders maintain basilisks in groups consisting of one male and two or three females. This alleviates the need to pair the animals at a specific time – they will generally start breeding shortly after the onset of the wet season.

With some luck, the female will become gravid (pregnant) shortly after the animals have bred. However, you may not notice that your female is gravid until she begins depositing eggs, so it is a good idea to go ahead and prepare for such an occurrence once you initiate the wet season.

Gravid females may alter their behavior in several subtle ways. They may begin frequenting the warmer portions of the habitat, or they may become more reclusive. After initially exhibiting an increased appetite, they may cease feeding as oviposition (egg deposition) approaches.

You'll have to provide females with a suitable egg-deposition chamber. A plastic storage container with an entry hole cut into the lid makes a suitable chamber. Fill the chamber about half-full with slightly damp sphagnum moss, potting soil or vermiculite.

Do not handle gravid females unless absolutely necessary, and try to keep their stress level as low as possible.

Egg Deposition and Recovery

If the female finds the egg chamber satisfactory, she will crawl into the container and dig a little tunnel in which she will lay her eggs. She will then produce up to 15 small eggs, before climbing back out of the chamber. She will often (but not always) recover the eggs with the substrate.

Once the female has deposited her eggs, begin trying to locate and retrieve the eggs. Use a gentle touch and take care not to damage the eggs.

Remove the eggs individually and place them in a deli cup or plastic food container, half-filled with slightly dampened vermiculite (most keepers use a 1:1 ratio of vermiculite to water, by weight) -- it should clump when compressed, but not release any water.

Avoid rotating the eggs while removing and transferring them to the egg chamber. Bury the eggs halfway into the vermiculite and close the container.

Egg Incubation

Basilisk eggs can be incubated in a number of different ways, but most keepers use an incubator, which allows you to set precise incubation temperatures.

You can purchase a commercially produced incubator or you can construct your own. Most any incubator designed for use with reptile eggs will suffice, but it is wise to test the unit and ensure it holds consistent temperatures before you are faced with eggs.

You can make your own incubator by filling a 10-gallon aquarium with a few inches of water. Place an aquarium heater in the water, and set the thermostat at the desired temperature. Place a brick in the water and rest the egg chamber on top of the brick. Cover the aquarium with a glass top to keep the heat and moisture contained.

Basilisk eggs will usually hatch between 1 and 3 months when incubated between 82 and 86 degrees Fahrenheit (27 to 30 degrees Celsius). The warmer the incubation temperature, the quicker the eggs will hatch, but the incubation temperature influences more than just the duration of the incubation period.

A juvenile basilisk.

Neonatal Husbandry

Once the young begin hatching from their eggs, you can remove them from the egg box and place them in a small cage or "nursery." Do not attempt to remove any hatchlings from their eggs. If any of the young emerge with their yolk sacs still attached, leave them in the egg box until they have absorbed the yolk.

A scaled-down version of an adult habitat, such as a small plastic storage box, makes a satisfactory nursery. Place several small pieces of crumpled paper or folded cardboard to provide the young with some form of cover.

Keep the nursery slightly more humid than the enclosure the adults live in, but the temperature gradient should be similar to that of the adults. You can initiate feeding trials within a day or two, but most will not begin to feed until after their first shed.

Chapter 16: Further Reading

Never stop learning more about your new pet's natural history, biology and captive care. This is the only way to ensure that you are providing your new pet with the highest quality of life possible.

It's always more fun to interact with your basilisk than to read about him, but by accumulating more knowledge, you'll be better able to provide him with a high quality of life.

Books

Bookstores and online book retailers offer a treasure trove of information that will advance your quest for knowledge. While books represent an additional cost involved in reptile care, you can consider it an investment in your pet's well-being. Your local library may also carry some books about basilisks, which you can borrow for no charge.

University libraries are a great place for finding old, obscure or academically oriented books about basilisks. You may not be allowed to borrow these books if you are not a student, but you can view and read them at the library.

Herpetology: An Introductory Biology of Amphibians and Reptiles
By Laurie J. Vitt, Janalee P. Caldwell
Top of Form
Bottom of Form
Academic Press, 2013

Understanding Reptile Parasites: A Basic Manual for Herpetoculturists & Veterinarians
By Roger Klingenberg D.V.M.
Advanced Vivarium Systems, 1997

Infectious Diseases and Pathology of Reptiles: Color Atlas and Text
Elliott Jacobson
CRC Press

Designer Reptiles and Amphibians
Richard D. Bartlett, Patricia Bartlett
Barron's Educational Series

Lizards: Windows to the Evolution of Diversity
By Eric R. Pianka, Laurie J. Vit

Magazines

Because magazines are typically published monthly or bi-monthly, they occasionally offer more up-to-date information than books do. Magazine articles are obviously not as comprehensive as books typically are, but they still have considerable value.

Reptiles Magazine
www.reptilesmagazine.com/
Covering reptiles commonly kept in captivity.

Practical Reptile Keeping
http://www.practicalreptilekeeping.co.uk/
Practical Reptile Keeping is a popular publication aimed at beginning and advanced hobbies. Topics include the care and maintenance of popular reptiles as well as information on wild reptiles.

Websites

The internet has made it much easier to find information about reptiles than it has ever been.

However, you must use discretion when deciding which websites to trust. While knowledgeable breeders, keepers and academics operate some websites, many who maintain reptile-oriented websites lack the same dedication and scientific rigor.

Anyone with a computer and internet connection can launch a website and say virtually anything they want about basilisks. Accordingly, as with all other research, consider the source of the information before making any husbandry decisions.

Note: at the time of printing, all the websites below were working. As the internet changes rapidly, some sites might no longer be live when you read this book. That is, of course, out of our control.

The Reptile Report
www.thereptilereport.com/
The Reptile Report is a news-aggregating website that accumulates interesting stories and features about reptiles from around the world.

Kingsnake.com
www.kingsnake.com
After starting as a small website for gray-banded kingsnake enthusiasts, Kingsnake.com has become one of the largest reptile-oriented portals in

the hobby. The site features classified advertisements, a breeder directory, message forums and other resources.

The Vivarium and Aquarium News
www.vivariumnews.com/
The online version of the former print publication, The Vivarium and Aquarium News provides in-depth coverage of different reptiles and amphibians in a captive and wild context.

Journals
Journals are the primary place professional scientists turn when they need to learn about basilisks. While they may not make light reading, hobbyists stand to learn a great deal from journals.

Herpetologica
www.hljournals.org/
Published by The Herpetologists' League, Herpetologica, and its companion publication, Herpetological Monographs cover all aspects of reptile and amphibian research.

Journal of Herpetology
www.ssarherps.org/
Produced by the Society for the Study of Reptiles and Amphibians, the Journal of Herpetology is a peer-reviewed publication covering a variety of reptile-related topics.

Copeia
www.asihcopeiaonline.org/
Copeia is published by the American Society of Ichthyologists and Herpetologists. A peer-reviewed journal, Copeia covers all aspects of the biology of reptiles, amphibians and fish.

Nature
www.nature.com/
Although Nature covers all aspects of the natural world, many issues contain information that lizard enthusiasts are sure to find interesting.

Supplies
You can obtain most of what you need to maintain basilisks through your local pet store, big-box retailer or hardware store, but online retailers offer another option.

Just be sure that you consider the shipping costs for any purchase, to ensure you aren't "saving" yourself a few dollars on the product, yet spending several more dollars to get the product delivered.

Big Apple Pet Supply
http://www.bigappleherp.com
Big Apple Pet Supply carries most common husbandry equipment, including heating devices, water dishes and substrates.

LLLReptile
http://www.lllreptile.com
LLL Reptile carries a wide variety of husbandry tools, heating devices, lighting products and more.

Support Organizations
Sometimes, the best way to learn about basilisks is to reach out to other keepers and breeders. Check out these organizations, and search for others in your geographic area.

The National Reptile & Amphibian Advisory Council
http://www.nraac.org/
The National Reptile & Amphibian Advisory Council seeks to educate the hobbyists, legislators and the public about reptile and amphibian related issues.

American Veterinary Medical Association
www.avma.org
The AVMA is a good place for Americans to turn if you are having trouble finding a suitable reptile veterinarian.

The World Veterinary Association
http://www.worldvet.org/
The World Veterinary Association is a good resource for finding suitable reptile veterinarians worldwide.

References

Abigail S. Tucker a, G. J. (2014). Evolution and developmental diversity of tooth regeneration. *Seminars in Cell & Developmental Biology*.

Anderson, S. P. (2003). The Phylogenetic Definition of Reptilia. *Systematic Biology*.

Christopher Vaughan, e. a. (2007). Home range and habitat use of Basiliscus plumifrons (Squamata: Corytophanidae) in an active Costa Rican cacao farm. *Applied Herpetology*.

Devender, R. W. (1978). Growth Ecology of a Tropical Lizard, Basiliscus basiliscus. *Ecology*.

Devender, R. W. (1982). Comparative Demography of the Lizard Basiliscus basiliscus. *Herpetologica*.

Fitch, R. R. (1974). Food Habits of Basiliscus basiliscus in Costa Rica. *Journal of Herpetology*.

MCMAHON, J. W. (1996). SIZE-DEPENDENCE OF WATER-RUNNING ABILITY IN BASILISK LIZARDS. *The Journal of Experimental Biology* .

Rand, A. S., & Marx, H. (1967). Running Speed of the Lizard Basiliscus basiliscus on Water. *Copeia*.